An Atlas of Papua and New Guinea

Edited/ **R Gerard Ward** Professor of Geography

David A M Lea Senior Lecturer in Geography

Cartography/Marlous Ploeg

Department of Geography
University of Papua and New Guinea
and Collins◇Longman

Collins ◊ Longman Atlases

Wm Collins Sons & Co Ltd Longman Group Ltd
144 Cathedral Street   Longman House Burnt Mill
Glasgow C4   Harlow Essex

First published 1970

ISBN 0 582 00081 5

Printed in Hong Kong by Yu Luen Offset Printing Factory

FOREWORD

Dr. J. T. Gunther, *C.M.G., O.B.E.*
Vice-Chancellor of the University of Papua & New Guinea

A good atlas is an essential tool not only of geographers but of economists, sociologists, political scientists and especially of educationalists and public health specialists. That the Reserve Bank of Australia and the Bank of New South Wales have given generous financial help to enable *An Atlas of Papua and New Guinea* to be published is surely an indication that an atlas of this nature is also thought to be needed equipment for financiers and commercial houses.

Whilst Professor Ward and Dr. Lea are from the University of Papua and New Guinea, they have sought widely to get the best scientific advice that is available. A great deal of help has come to them not only from the Australian National University, and especially from its New Guinea Research Unit, but also from members of Commonwealth Government Departments and the Administration. This is a worthy document, therefore, to be put before such a grandly cosmopolitan Association as ANZAAS.

The University is proud that its Department of Geography has shown the initiative and produced an atlas that I would highly recommend.

PREFACE
Professor H. C. Brookfield
Pennsylvania State University

Two decades constitute a long period in the history of a developing country, and it is a measure of enormous progress, both of Papua and New Guinea itself, and of scientific research in the Territory, to compare the present *Atlas of Papua and New Guinea* with its only predecessor, the *Resource Atlas of Papua and New Guinea* prepared in 1951. The widened range of maps, the enormously greater wealth and depth of information, the enhanced detail and accuracy of representation, all bear witness to the scale and span of the research effort, and to the improvement in mapping, data collection and statistical coverage, which has gone hand-in-hand with scientific progress. Even one decade ago it would have been quite impossible to produce an atlas on anything like the present scale, and it is clear that we are currently on a rising curve in the accumulation and refinement of scientific knowledge about this Territory. The present *Atlas* represents, as it were, a 'snapshot' of the stage of progress in our understanding of New Guinea: it is to the great credit of the compilers in the young University of Papua and New Guinea, and of the contributors, that so impressive a collection of information has been prepared. Much of the material presented is a compilation of work carried out by academic research workers, and by government and semi-government bodies—outstandingly the Division of Land Research at C.S.I.R.O., but there is in addition a number of wholly new maps, prepared from existing data not previously collected together, or interpreted in the ways here essayed. The result of this latter contribution is a better-balanced collection, presenting comprehensive data on population, history and settlement, natural environment, and productive and tertiary activities.

What emerges most strikingly from these maps is the great diversity of the country. The physical diversity has been remarked from earliest times, and it here emerges very clearly in maps of landform, rainfall, and land-use potential. The great unevenness of population distribution is also evident: nearly half the total population lives in a restricted belt lying close to the parallel of 6° south, mainly at high altitudes. This imbalance in inherited distribution may be compared with the uneven distribution of the cash economy—the true degree of which does not always emerge from a reading of the official and semi-popular literature, but which is here strikingly displayed in a series of maps of production, infrastructure and services. The resulting discordance is reflected in the pattern of internal migration, of resettlement, and of efforts to spread the distribution of development through provision of services, and of loans. All this and much more can be gleaned from a careful study of the *Atlas*.

This is perhaps the greatest single value of such a compilation as the present, at such a time as this. Papua and New Guinea is undergoing the most rapid of transformations from being a little-developed colonial dependency with a 'fringe' cash economy, into an emergent nation of more integrated economy, based on a new pattern of resource use, and structured by means of a new transport system through ports and towns that are the most rapid growth-centres in the country. A new appraisal and evaluation of resources is an essential part of this change, which is leading to a complete reconstruction of the 'map' of relative economic values of different areas and locations. This spatial aspect of the development process, too often neglected, is of major importance, and the present *Atlas* is a mine of source material to aid in its understanding. Just as we can see here the relationship between the pattern of development and that of resources, or of indigenous population, so also we can see evidence of Myrdal's 'circular causation' process, whereby the inequalities between areas created through development tend to become self-reinforcing, and this despite conscious efforts in this Territory to achieve a more 'uniform' distribution of the benefits of change.

The value of this *Atlas* is self-evident, but its production may also carry another message. Collected cartographic representation of a range of data has been recognised to be of high utility in a great many countries since World War II, and the result has been a series of National Atlas productions of great value in planning, in the framing of policy, and in education in its broadest sense. The compilers of this *Atlas* would not claim that their work is more than a step in the direction of such a National Atlas for Papua and New Guinea, but they have surely demonstrated the feasibility and potential utility of such an enterprise. It seems paradoxical to express the hope that so excellent a production will have a short life, but in a fast-changing New Guinea it is highly desirable that it should soon be replaced. One hopes, therefore, that the planning of a true National Atlas of this varied, fascinating and important developing country will not now be long delayed, and that the present work will serve an important role in bringing about the production of a detailed and comprehensive atlas that will aid in the emergence of an independent New Guinea.

LIST OF MAPS

LIST OF COMMENTARIES

ACKNOWLEDGEMENTS

This *Atlas* has been prepared to mark the occasion of the 42nd ANZAAS Congress held in Port Moresby during 1970. It is hoped that it will serve as an introduction to Papua and New Guinea for Congress visitors and also as a useful collection of material for others interested in the country. This is the first attempt to present so much data on Papua and New Guinea in cartographic form. Many other useful maps might have been included but data were not available or there was insufficient time to retrieve the necessary information before the *Atlas* went to press. The editors hope that readers will send criticisms and suggestions so that the *Atlas* may be improved, expanded and brought up to date from time to time.

The *Atlas* is the result of the voluntary efforts of a large number of contributors, and the editors wish to thank them for their enthusiasm and co-operation in meeting almost impossible deadlines. We also appreciate the work of Mrs. Marlous Ploeg who drew all the maps for the *Atlas* in addition to maintaining the Department of Geography's cartographic unit. We would like to thank the New Guinea Organising Committee of ANZAAS, under the Chairmanship of Dr. R. F. R. Scragg, for accepting the idea of an *Atlas of Papua and New Guinea* and for supporting and helping us throughout. Acknowledgement should also be made to the University of Papua and New Guinea for assisting in many ways.

It is impractical to name all to whom thanks are due, but special mention must be made of Mrs. J. Crimmins and Mrs. P. Barnes for typing numerous drafts; Mrs. Susan Pain for checking manuscripts, drafting some maps and collating data; Mr. C. Freeman, New Guinea Librarian of the University of Papua and New Guinea, for finding information; and Mrs. S. Drinkrow of the University of Papua and New Guinea and Mr. J. Dekker of the Department of Information and Extension Services for help with photographic work. In addition to those who contributed as authors, numerous officers in the Departments of the Administrator, Agriculture, Stock and Fisheries, Education, Forestry, Trade and Industries and in the Bureau of Statistics assisted with facts and figures. Finally we would like to thank our colleagues in the Department of Geography, University of Papua and New Guinea, for their help, advice and criticism.

Generous grants which enabled the *Atlas* to be published for the ANZAAS Congress were made by:

Australian Consolidated Industries Limited
Australian Mutual Provident Society
Bank of New South Wales
Broken Hill Proprietary Company Limited
Colonial Sugar Refining Company Limited
Mapmakers Proprietary Limited
Reserve Bank of Australia
Steamships Trading Company Limited

R. Gerard Ward and David A. M. Lea
University of Papua and New Guinea

INTRODUCTION TO POPULATION

R. GERARD WARD

The population of Papua and New Guinea, consisting of 2,150,317 indigenes and 34,669 non-indigenes, is incredibly diverse in almost every characteristic. The first section of the *Atlas* portrays some of this diversity though, as various authors point out, our knowledge of many aspects is still very imperfect. Nevertheless, as Maps 3 a–b and 4 a–b indicate, the area of unknown territory has been steadily reduced during the present century until today only very small pockets are truly "unexplored". As administration was extended into the interior (Maps 3 a–b and 4 a–b) in the 1930s the country's largest concentrations of population were discovered (Map 5) and during the 1950s were brought under administrative control (Map 4b). As this process continued the need to reorganize administrative structures was reflected in increases in the number of administrative districts and in rationalization of their boundaries. Changes since 1946 are shown in Maps 2 a–d.

The processes of socio-economic change initiated by contact with Europeans and other aliens have accelerated markedly in recent years and their effects have diffused towards the remotest parts of the country. Unfortunately, statistics are rarely available to enable the temporal changes to be portrayed in map form. However, many maps in this and subsequent sections do show (e.g. Maps 7, 8, 32, 44 and 47) regional variations in intensity of the impact at the present time. As knowledge of other areas penetrates to hitherto isolated communities, and the desire to obtain new goods and services increases, greater numbers of indigenes are leaving their home villages and subsistence economies and moving, temporarily or permanently, to areas of commercial activity. Maps 7 a–b and 8 a–b give some indication of the degree of commercial penetration in different areas and of the internal migration which results as people reappraise the relative advantages offered by different parts of their country.

In a country which has such a great linguistic diversity in relation to population and size (Maps 9 and 10) the processes of administrative unification, widening economic opportunities and migration have necessitated the development of lingue franche, and no less than twelve of these have been fostered by government, missions and employers, and spread by the indigenous people themselves (Map 11).

Prior to 1941 the pattern of Christian mission activity in Papua and New Guinea was fairly simple with each denomination having a relatively discrete sphere of influence (Map 12). But since 1946 many new denominations have entered the mission field and today the situation is much more complex. Indeed, the detail is too complicated to portray in full on a map at the scale available in this *Atlas* and Map 13 shows only the first-ranking denomination of each area, with that of second rank indicated in some places.

It might be argued that the work of missions has added both good and bad features to the changing cultures of Papua and New Guinea and the same is true of the impact of the alien culture on the distribution of disease in the country. The incidence of tuberculosis has increased with greater contact and migration and the variation in present incidence is closely related to urbanization and the degree of commercialization in rural areas. On the other hand, other diseases such as leprosy and yaws are being brought under partial or almost complete control, while the extension of health services and public health programmes, such as malaria control, are now resulting in rapidly rising rates of population increase.

At the present time the distribution of population (Map 5) and the variations in density (Map 6) are still predominantly reflections of the interaction between traditional subsistence economic systems and the variable habitat potential of the physical environment (Maps 18–28). But increasingly the distribution of population will change under the impact of economic, social and medical innovations.

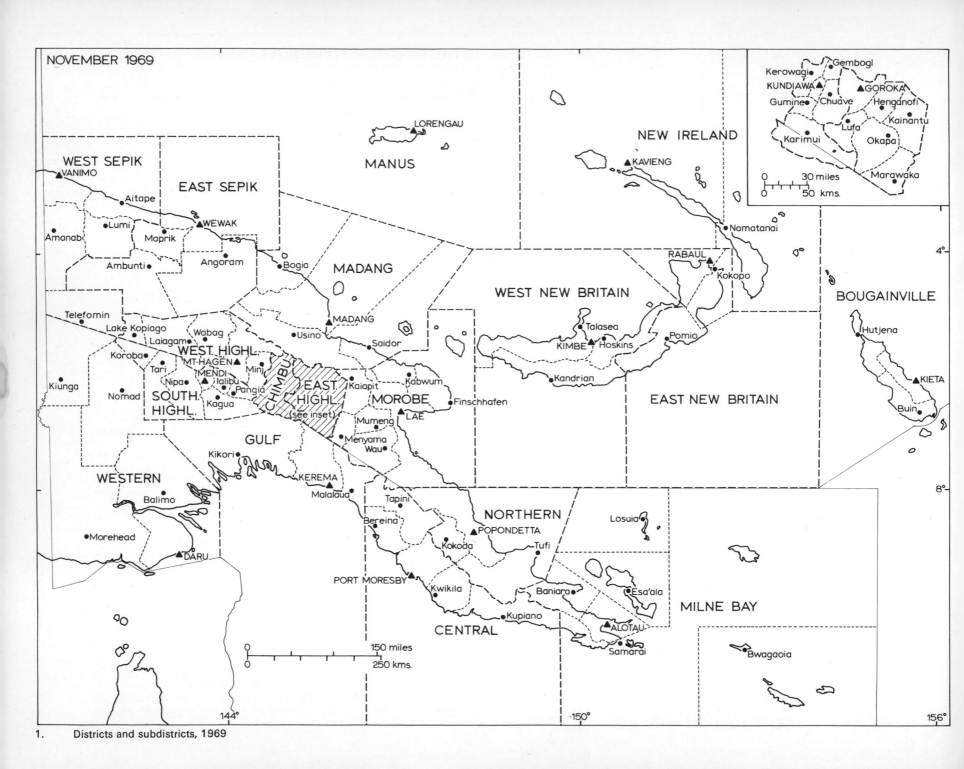

1.   Districts and subdistricts, 1969

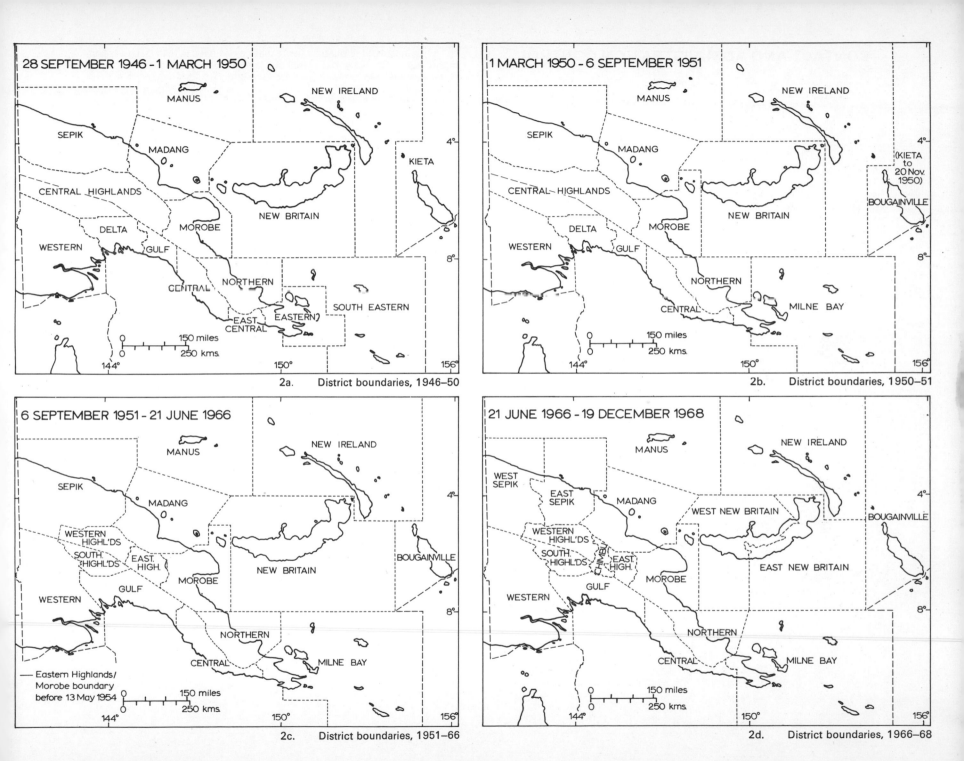

2a. District boundaries, 1946–50

2b. District boundaries, 1950–51

2c. District boundaries, 1951–66

2d. District boundaries, 1966–68

CONTACT AND ADMINISTRATION CONTROL

H. NELSON *

In 1873 Captain John Moresby wrote that he had filled in the "last great blank" in the work of the early navigators by "laying down the outlines of East New Guinea on the map of the world". Cartographers could now mark the coast of New Guinea with a firmer line, but the interior remained unknown to the outside world. Only those peaks visible from the coast had been named by Europeans. When D'Albertis published a map in 1880 to illustrate his travels he assumed that the ranges he had observed at the head of the Fly formed a backbone to the island; a continuation of the ranges seen in the east. Until the 1930s it remained a common assumption that towards the centre of New Guinea the mountains became more broken and precipitous, and the population more sparse.

* Lecturer in History, University of Papua and New Guinea.

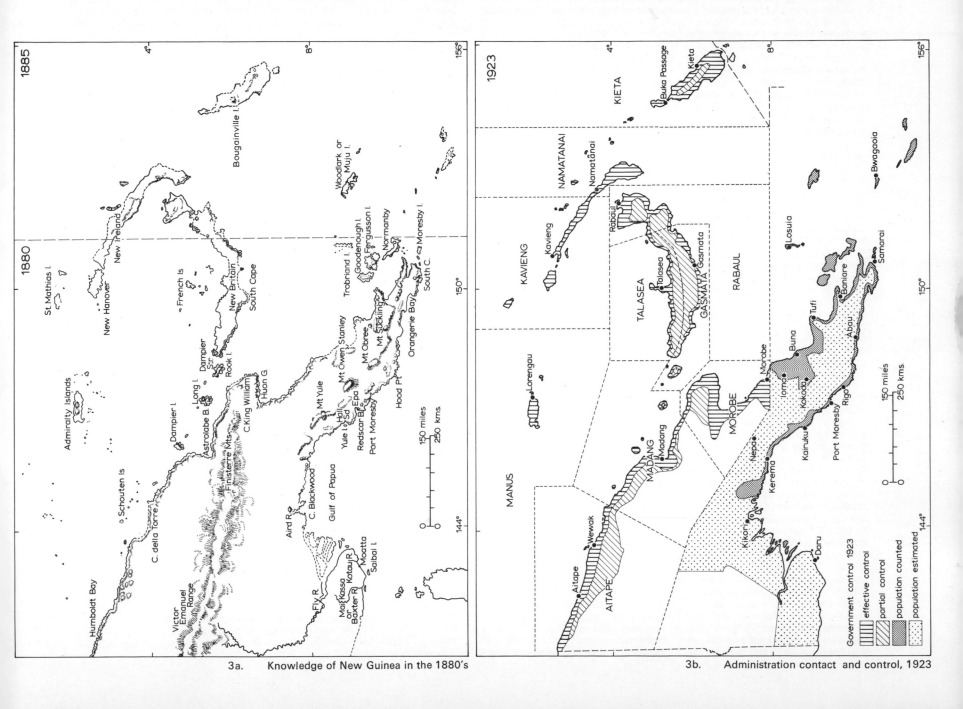

1885
1880

St Mathias I.

New Hanover

New Ireland

Bougainville I.

Admiralty Islands

French Is

Dampier I.

Long I.

Dampier Str.

Rook I.

New Britain

South Cape

Woodlark or Muju I.

Schouten Is

Humboldt Bay

Astrolabe B.

Huon G.

C King William

Finisterre Mts

Victor Emanuel Range

C. della Torre

Trobriand I.

Goodenough I.

Fergusson I.

Normanby

Mt Obree

Mt Suckling

Mt Owen Stanley

Mt Yule

Hall Sd

Epa

Yule I.

Redscar B.

Port Moresby

C. Blackwood

Aird R.

Gulf of Papua

Fly R.

Mai Kossa or Baxter R.

Kotau R.

Moatta

Saibai I.

Hood Pt

Orangerie Bay

Moresby I.

South C.

4°

8°

2°

156°

150°

144°

6°

150 miles

250 kms.

3a.   Knowledge of New Guinea in the 1880's

1923

KIETA

Buka Passage

Kieta

NAMATANAI

Namatanai

KAVIENG

Kavieng

Rabaul

TALASEA

Talasea

GASMATA

Gasmata

RABAUL

Bwagaoia

Losuia

Samarai

Baniare

Tufi

MANUS

Lorengau

Abau

Buna

Morobe

Ioma

MOROBE

Kokoda

Rigo

Port Moresby

MADANG

Madang

Nepa

Kainuku

Kerema

AITAPE

Aitape

Wewok

Kikori

Daru

4°

8°

6°

2°

156°

150°

144°

Government control 1923

effective control

partial control

population counted

population estimated

150 miles

250 kms.

3b.   Administration contact and control, 1923

The Australian Administration's first *Report* to the League of Nations included a map showing the areas under "effective" and "partial" government control. This showed much of the interior of Bougainville, New Britain and the mainland as beyond all government influence and unknown to map-makers. The *Report* estimated that over 27 per cent of the total area of the Mandated Territory was still "known only from such glimpses as can be had from a passing ship or from a distant peak". Only on the lower Sepik, the Huon Gulf and the Gazelle Peninsula were there mission stations or government posts more than 10 miles from the coast.

In spite of the restriction of the controlled area to the coast in 1923, there had been some penetration of the interior. After Dr. O. Finsch entered the mouth of the Sepik in 1885, there were a number of expeditions up the river. In the next two years G. E. G. Von Schleinitz and Dr. C. Schader both travelled beyond Ambunti; then in 1910 and 1912–13 expeditions under L. Schultze and W. Behrmann passed the point where the Sepik crosses the West Irian border to map the country of the Sepik headwaters and some of its tributaries. In the east scientists, prospectors, government officials and Lutheran missionaries explored the Huon Peninsula and traced the valleys of the Ramu, Markham, Watut, Bulolo and Waria Rivers. Matt Crowe, Frank Pryke and Arthur Darling were probably the best known of the prospectors. In some cases the prospectors had entered German New Guinea illegally from the Northern Division of Papua, but after 1906 it was possible to obtain permission from the German administration to prospect in German territory. In 1913 the Lutheran missionaries, Georg Pilhofer and Leonhardt Flierl went up the Waria River, crossed into the valleys of the Bulolo and the Watut, and then descended the Markham. Pilhofer published an account of the expedition; the movements of the miners generally went unrecorded. During the period of administration by the Australian military forces from 1914 to 1921 the area under effective government control was not extended and in some areas may have contracted.

The legend accompanying the 1923 map of Papua did not claim that the shaded area indicated government control, but the map is still misleading. The population living to the east of the Strickland River (including what is now the Southern Highlands) had not been "estimated" and in other areas only the roughest guesses had been made. In 1920 Assistant Resident Magistrate Muscutt reported from the neglected and soon to be abandoned outpost of Nepa "that very little progress had been made in civilizing of the Kuku-kuku natives". His report noted that he had received mail only five times in the preceding 14 months. In 1921 the Central District Resident Magistrate admitted that the Goilala area "cannot be said to be under control". Other maps printed at the time indicate those areas known to the outside world by the early 1920s. A period of active patrolling started by Murray just before 1914 had filled in most of the detail on the map east of Cape Possession, but to the west the upper Purari and Kikori Rivers were unmarked. The Fly and the Strickland had provided two lines of entry into the far northwest. Gold had led to the establishment of the only inland government stations of Nepa and Kokoda.

In 1939 Sir Hubert Murray wrote, "we may now say that the whole of Papua has been explored. Doubtless there are nooks and crannies and small patches of land here and there in the main range and elsewhere which have not been visited . . . but we can, I think, safely say that there is no large village and no extensive district in Papua which has not been visited". C. Karius and I. Champion had explored the upper Fly and Strickland areas in 1927 and 1928 before finding their way to the Sepik. In 1930 M. Leahy and M. Dwyer on a prospecting expedition in the Mandated Territory crossed into Papua and descended the Purari; "a good piece of bushmanship" said Murray. The area between the Strickland and the upper Purari was crossed by J. Hides and J. O'Malley in 1935 and the next year I. Champion and C. T. J. Adamson again travelled east on a patrol from the Bamu to the Purari. C. Champion and F. Adamson cut north across the two previous patrols in 1937 from Kikori to Lake Kutubu and on to the north and east into the Mandated Territory. Lake Kutubu then became the centre for further patrolling in the Papuan Highlands. Murray could be fairly confident in 1939 when he proclaimed the end of Papuan exploration for by that time much of the Territory had been seen from the air.

More extensive use had been made of aircraft in the Mandated Territory, but there too most work had to be done on foot. Before Leahy and Dwyer crossed the island in 1930 Lutheran missionaries and miners had gained an idea of the real nature of the Highlands by penetrating the country beyond Kainantu. L. Flierl probably entered the valley of the Bena Bena in 1926; he certainly learnt of the populated valleys of the area. Three years later Pilhofer and Wilhelm Bergmann travelled down the Dunantina and then turned west to reach the Bena Bena. At the same time as Pilhofer and Bergmann were confirming the reports made by Flierl, the prospector, Ned Rowlands, had established a camp near Kainantu. Rumours of Rowlands' activities encouraged Leahy and Dwyer to enter the area in 1930. G. W. L. Townsend, District Officer in the Sepik, believed that the recruiter and miner, William MacGregor, entered the Western Highlands from the Sepik in 1929–30, but there is little supporting evidence. The Leahy brothers assisted by finance from New Guinea Goldfields Company built an airstrip at Bena Bena and from there in 1933 a party flew over the Chimbu and Wahgi Valleys. That flight, Leahy wrote, "laid to rest for all time the theory that the Centre of New Guinea is a mass of uninhabitable mountains". The most prolonged of the subsequent patrols were those by M. Leahy and J. Taylor in 1933 and J. Taylor and J. Black in 1938 and 1939.

The extension of government control was shown to the League of Nations by the advance of the shaded areas into the Highlands and by the growth in the "Enumerated Population" from 187,517 in 1921 to 400,135 and 627,283 in 1930 and 1939 respectively. The neat but arbitrary fourfold classification showing the degree of government control in the Mandated Territory was not used by the Papuan administration.

The *Uncontrolled Areas Ordinance* came into effect in the Mandated Territory in 1926. Under the *Ordinance* people other than New Guineans and Administration Officers could not enter an area said to be Uncontrolled without a permit. No similar law was introduced in Papua until 1936 when over 13,000 square miles between the Strickland and the 144° Meridian were proclaimed under the *Uncontrolled Area Ordinance*. The Papuan regulations had no provision for permits: miners, missionaries and others were to be kept out of the "wonderland" described by Hides. Until the passing of the 1936 *Ordinance* the existence of Uncontrolled Areas in the Mandated Territory had been seen as one of the differences in approach of the two administrations. On 1st July 1939, Sir Hubert Murray removed all restrictions on entry into the area defined in 1936. The *Restricted Areas Ordinance* was passed in 1950 and first used in 1951 when a proclamation revoked the boundaries defined under the New Guinea *Uncontrolled Areas Ordinance* and re-imposed restrictions of entry on an area of Papua. Since 1951 the Restricted Areas have been progressively reduced. In mid-1969 there were two Restricted Areas: in the northwest of the Western Highlands and in the southwest of the West Sepik District. Approximately 2,300 people lived in the Restricted Areas.

Bibliography

Souter, G., 1963. *New Guinea: The Last Unknown.* Sydney

Murray, J. H. P., 1923. *Recent Exploration in Papua.* Sydney

Willis, I., 1969. "Who was First?": *Journal of the Papua and New Guinea Society*, Vol. 3, No. 1

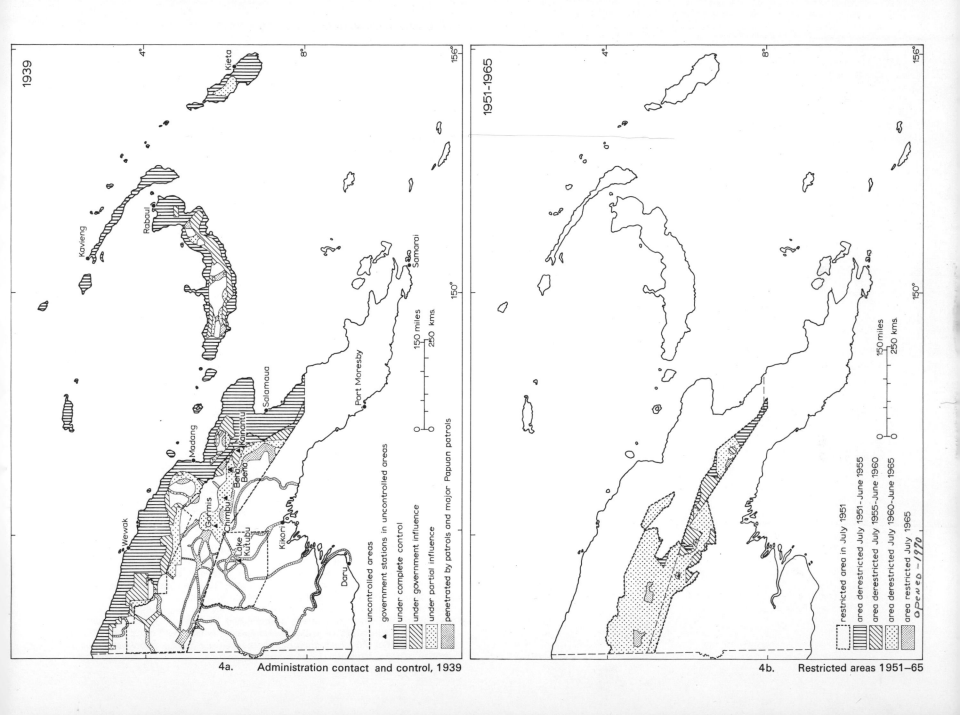

4a.   Administration contact and control, 1939

4b.   Restricted areas 1951–65

Map 4a (1939):

1939

Kieta

Kavieng

Rabaul

Samarai

Wewak

Madang

Salamaua

Gormis

Chimbu

Bena

Benq

Kainantu

Lake Kutubu

Kikori

Port Moresby

Daru

150 miles
250 kms.

Legend:
- - - uncontrolled areas
▲ government stations in uncontrolled areas
under complete control
under government influence
under partial influence
penetrated by patrols and major Papuan patrols

Map 4b (1951–1965):

1951-1965

150 miles
250 kms.

Legend:
restricted area in July 1951
area derestricted July 1951–June 1955
area derestricted July 1955–June 1960
area derestricted July 1960–June 1965
area restricted July 1965

OPENED – 1970

DISTRIBUTION AND DENSITY OF POPULATION

R. GERARD WARD

Prior to 1966, only partial censuses had been conducted in Papua and New Guinea. The indigenous population was counted once in from one to three years by census patrols of the Department of Native Affairs and its successor, the Department of District Administration. These *de jure* counts in villages, were of considerable value though of variable reliability, and did not cover urban or plantation areas. The expatriate population was enumerated concurrently with the Australian censuses. The census of June–July 1966 was the first attempt to cover both sectors and it provided a complete enumeration of urban and non-village areas (e.g. plantations, missions, government stations) and a sample of village areas. The enumeration was *de facto* except for members of the census teams. As the data from the sample section of the census cannot be disaggregated below district level, Maps 5 and 6 have been based on the 1966 census with additional distributional information from D.D.A. counts. Map 5 is based on a manuscript map at 1:1,000,000 prepared in 1969 by K. J. Granger, Department of Forests. The 1:1,000,000 map was itself based on 18 district maps of population distribution (at various larger scales) prepared by the same author.

In order to avoid the distortions of density which result from the use of administrative units of uneven size and shape, the population distribution map at 1:1,000,000 was gridded with 100 square mile grid squares and densities calculated for each square. Map 6 has been drawn from these data.

The distribution of population in Papua and New Guinea is extremely uneven. In some areas the basic explanation of this unevenness lies in the variable potential of the environment for use under subsistence cultivation of roots and other crops (Maps 30 and 31). But in many areas the population density is well below that which the environment might support under this form of economy. It appears that the population had not reached a stable distribution by the time European contact, innovations and new forms of economy inaugurated a process of major redistribution which continues today. Only 18·6 per cent of the total indigenous work force is wholly or mainly engaged in money raising, and the location of commercial activity is the dominant

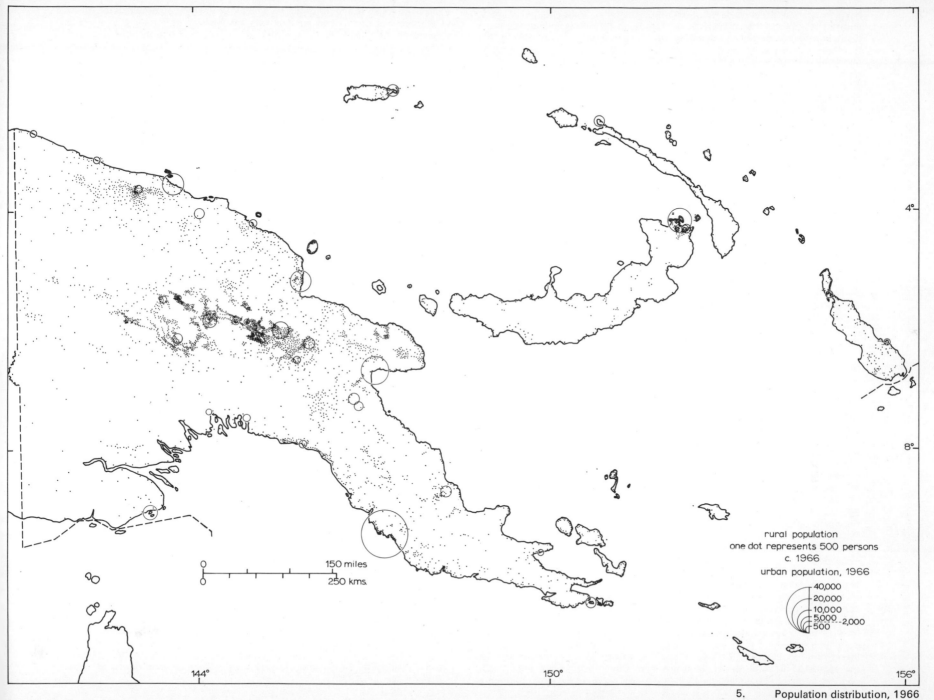

rural population
one dot represents 500 persons
c. 1966

urban population, 1966

40,000
20,000
10,000
5,000 --2,000
500

150 miles

250 kms.

5.   Population distribution, 1966

determinant of population distribution only in the urban areas and their vicinity, and in those parts of East New Britain, Bougainville, New Ireland and other districts where expatriate plantations are most numerous. Nevertheless, the distribution is changing at an increasing rate and the commercial sector of the economy will influence the location of an increasing proportion of the population.

The major concentrations of rural population are in the valleys of the Eastern Highlands, Chimbu, Western Highlands and Southern Highlands districts which together have 39 per cent of the country's people. Throughout these districts, the sweet potato (*Ipomoea batatas*) is the staple crop (Map 31) and skilful cultivation and favourable soils and climate are the bases of population densities which rise locally to 500 per square mile. Local variations in the suitability of the environment for sweet potato cultivation greatly influence local patterns of population distribution. Above about 7,000 ft. the tubers take significantly longer to mature and the risk of frost damage increases. Though some communities counter this by composting and other techniques, the effects of increasing altitudes and steeper slopes on sweet potato yield are the dominant causes of the sharp upper boundaries of the Highland population concentrations. At the time of first European contact, and since, the lower parts of many of the highland basins were thinly populated. The often abrupt lower margin of dense settlement is apparently due to the combined effects of low rainfall, the establishment of anthropogenic short grassland and depleted soils (following cultivation and frequent fires), warfare and disease, probably including malaria (Brookfield, 1964).

Outside the Highlands, the most important inland area with a high population density is in the Maprik subdistrict of East Sepik where a mixed economy of yam, taro and sago cultivation supports densities of over 160 persons per square mile (rising locally to 400 per square mile). Rural densities of over 160 per square mile also occur in the Gazelle Peninsula where large scale land alienation before 1914 and rapid population growth since 1945 amongst the Tolai have brought considerable population pressure. The volcanic ash soils of this area are intensively cultivated for both food and cash crops. Most of the remaining small concentrations of dense population are close to the coasts where pockets of fertile volcanic or alluvial soils occur and where sea food supplements garden produce. Nevertheless some areas with these physical characteristics have virtually no population, as for example in parts of the Cape Hoskins area. Large areas of Western District and West and East Sepik have very little population. In the former, much of the land is swampy though lowland rainforest covers considerable areas which are at present almost unoccupied even though topographically suitable for agriculture (Map 28). In West and East Sepik the extensive swamp lands are thinly peopled while the main axial ranges of Papua and New Britain have low densities due to the small proportion of land suitable for agriculture.

Between the areas with extremes of density lies the bulk of the country having up to 40 persons per square mile. Local variations in agricultural or gathering systems are partly responsible for differing densities, but in general most areas (outside parts of Chimbu District and Wabag and East Sepik subdistricts) could support greater rural densities under subsistence agriculture than they do today. As agriculture becomes more commercial, however, the increased demand for land for cash crops, and the more selective ecological requirements of these crops are likely to bring population pressure into more rural areas.

In most rural areas the nucleated village with fragmented garden holdings is the dominant settlement unit. Villages rarely have more than 300 or 400 people though the populations of those adjacent to towns have often been swollen by migrants. In some areas, missions and Government have encouraged concentration into larger villages than in pre-contact times for ease of adminis-tration.Elsewhere examples of the reverse tendency may be noted as the threat of warfare has been removed and villagers have begun to live in a more dispersed pattern. In parts of the Highlands hamlets and dispersed houses, and sometimes separate men's and women's houses, are the rule, while in Western District the longhouse is characteristic of some areas. The form of rural settlement varies greatly but in many areas it has been modified considerably since European contact.

In 1966 only 5·9 per cent of the total population were living in towns but the rate of increase in urban areas is much faster than that of the country as a whole. It is estimated that Port Moresby's population is increasing at about six per cent per year against a national figure of 2·2 per cent (van de Kaa, 1970). The other major towns are probably experiencing similar high rates of growth. Table 1 gives the population of all towns with over 2,000 people. As Map 5 shows, the five largest towns are all coastal and all are major ports. Their location, together with that of most of the smaller coastal towns, was greatly influenced by the availability of satisfactory anchorages. Today each of the main coastal towns acts as a distribution, service and administrative centre while the larger ones are attracting more light industries. Port Moresby is more than double the size of the second town, Lae, and its pre-eminence is primarily due to its role as capital and centre of administration for the country. With over two and a half times as many non-indigenes as any other town (many being Government employees) Port Moresby is the largest high-income market in the country and therefore has attracted more secondary and service industries than any other centre.

As indicated in Table 1, all towns have a dominant indigenous population but whereas only 4·8 per cent of indigenes were urban dwellers in 1966, 70·4 per cent of non-indigenes lived in towns. The indigenous urban population has an extremely unbalanced sex ratio with 183 males per 100 females.

Table 1
Population of Main Towns, June–July 1966

	Indigenous	Non-Indigenous	Total
Port Moresby	31,983	9,865	41,848
Lae	13,341	3,205	16,546
Rabaul	6,925	3,636	10,561
Wewak	7,967	978	8,945
Madang	7,398	1,439	8,837
Goroka	3,890	936	4,826
Daru	3,444	219	3,663
Mount Hagen	2,764	551	3,315
Bulolo	2,245	479	2,724
Lorengau	2,100	346	2,446
Samarai	1,699	502	2,201
Kavieng	1,707	435	2,142
Popondetta	1,844	295	2,139

Source: Bureau of Statistics, n.d. : 8

Bibliography

Brookfield, H. C., 1960. "Population Distribution and Labour Migration in New Guinea", *Australian Geographer,* Vol. 6, pp 233–42.

Brookfield, H. C., 1964. "The Ecology of Highland Settlement: Some Suggestions", *American Anthropologist,* Vol. 66, pp 20–38.

Bureau of Statistics, n.d. (1968). *Population Census, 1966 Preliminary Bulletin,* No. 20, Port Moresby.

van de Kaa, D. J., 1970. "Estimates of Vital Rates and Future Growth in People and Planning in Papua and New Guinea", *New Guinea Research Unit Bulletin,* No. 34, 1970.

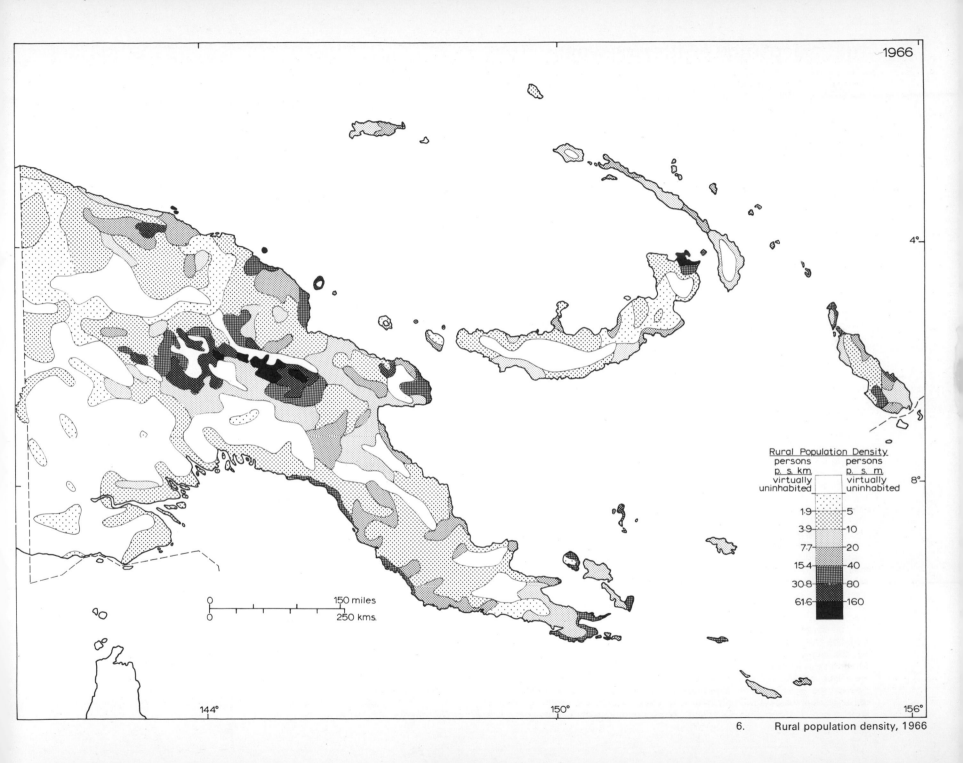

Rural Population Density

persons p. s. km.	persons p. s. m.
virtually uninhabited	virtually uninhabited
1.9	5
3.9	10
7.7	20
15.4	40
30.8	80
61.6	160

150 miles

250 kms.

6.   Rural population density, 1966

THE COMPOSITION OF THE WORKFORCE

R. GERARD WARD

The workforce of Papua and New Guinea may be classified according to the amount of involvement in the monetary sector, and regional variation in this is of considerable economic importance. The range is from an entirely subsistence and non-monetary agriculture, hunting or fishing economy, to complete dependence on earned cash income and with every possible combination between. Therefore the categories used in the compilation of the Census and in Map 7a cannot be precisely defined. In mid-1966 18·6 per cent of the total indigenous workforce were in the "wholly or mainly money-raising sector" and 46·2 per cent in the "wholly subsistence" sector. The remainder were partly involved in money-raising.

The regional differences in the relative importance of the three sectors clearly indicates the variation in the degree of penetration by the commercial economy. East New Britain and Central District with 46 and 41·5 per cent respectively are the only districts with over one-third of their workforces "wholly or mainly money-raising". In Central District this reflects the relatively high proportion of urban population while in East New Britain the large plantation workforce and the well developed cash crop economy of the Tolai people are the principal factors. At the other extreme are West Sepik, Southern Highlands, Western, Gulf and Milne Bay, none of which have over 12 per cent in the "wholly or mainly money-raising" sector, or under 60 per cent in the "wholly subsistence" sector. Difficulties of internal transport; the absence of non-indigenous commercial activity; and the relatively late penetration of parts of the districts by administration services are all contributory factors. The low level of commercial activity in these districts is one reason for their role as net exporters of labour (Map 8a). It is also notable that the same districts have low rankings in terms of many other indicators of economic activity (e.g. Maps 32, 34, 38 and 41) and availability of social services (e.g. Map 43).

Most districts with a significant "wholly or mainly money-raising" sector also have a large proportion of workers in the transitional sector in which subsistence production is supplemented by some monetary income. This generally represents agriculturalists who have added cash cropping to their subsistence gardens. Chimbu District is outstanding with 72 per cent of its workforce in this category. Most of these will be coffee growers but the figure is so high in comparison with other districts that there may also have been some enumerator bias in this district.

Occupations of the Money-Raising Workforce

The money-raising workforce (equivalent to the combined "wholly or mainly money-raising" and "mainly subsistence with some money-raising") is subdivided by occupation in Map 7b. Considerable difficulties were experienced in the 1966 Census in classifying the workforce by occupation and the resulting statistics must be used and interpreted with caution (Bureau of Statistics, n.d.: 50). Nevertheless the general situation is clearly revealed in Map 7b.

Farming, forestry and fishing is the overwhelming occupation with Central District (50·5 per cent) being the only district in which the proportion falls below 66 per cent of the total indigenous money-raising workforce. For the whole of Papua and New Guinea, 87 per cent of the indigenous money-raising workforce are engaged in these occupations. This figure understates the total importance of primary industry as virtually all those in the subsistence sector (Map 7a) are farmers. Of the total indigenous workforce an estimated 90 per cent are engaged in farming, forestry and fishing.

It is only in the main towns that craft and industrial employment is significant and only in Central District (Port Moresby), where 22 per cent are so engaged, does the proportion exceed 15 per cent of the money-raising workforce. The two Army barracks and large number of domestic servants within Port Moresby account for the relatively high 'services' component. Most other occupation groups show little regional variation, a fact which reflects the relatively small development of non-agricultural activity and the uniformity of administrative functions in all districts. The 1971 census will no doubt show a great change in the employment pattern on Bougainville with the further development of copper mining.

Bibliography:

Bureau of Statistics, n.d. (1968). *Population Census, 1966, Preliminary Bulletin No. 20,* Port Moresby.

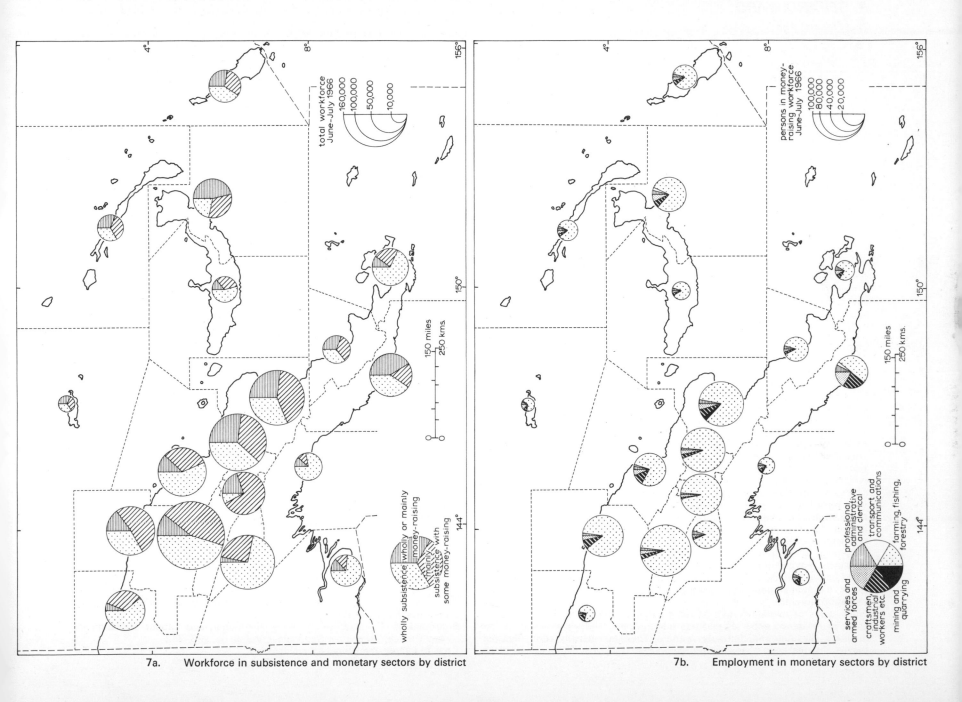

7a.   Workforce in subsistence and monetary sectors by district

7b.   Employment in monetary sectors by district

total workforce
June–July 1966

160,000
100,000
50,000
10,000

wholly subsistence

wholly or mainly
money-raising

mainly
subsistence with
some money-raising

150 miles
250 kms

persons in money-
raising workforce
June–July 1966

100,000
80,000
40,000
20,000

150 miles
250 kms.

professional,
administrative
and clerical

transport and
communications

services and
armed forces

farming, fishing,
forestry

craftsmen,
industrial
workers etc.

mining and
quarrying

INTERNAL MIGRATION

R. GERARD WARD

with relatively short contact with administration, much of the out-migration is under the agreement labour system. Men are recruited (by licenced recruiters or, in the Highlands, by administration officers) to engage for two-year contracts on plantations or with other employers. Fares to the place of employment are paid by the employer and workers are repatriated at the end of their contracts. Remuneration is partly in cash and partly in issues of rations, clothing and other requirements. In 1967, only about one-third of male workers in the money-raising sector were employed under agreements, compared with about 55 per cent in 1959–60 (Dept. of Labour). The main sources of agreement workers are now Southern, Eastern and Western Highlands and West Sepik. As alternative sources of income develop within any area the number of agreement workers declines, both because of local cash-earning opportunities and because potential migrants are able to pay their own fares and thus avoid signing agreements. The main destinations for agreement workers are coconut and cocoa plantations in East New Britain, New Ireland and Bougainville, tea and coffee plantations in Western Highlands and rubber plantations in Central District.

The third major type of migration is by individuals making their own way to employment centres to find work as "casual labour". Such workers are not bound by agreements and are free to choose and change their employers. This is the main type of migration to the urban areas and, increasingly, to plantations and other centres of rural employment.

The main sources of internal migrants are generally those districts with little non-indigenous economic activity and where indigenous cash-cropping is little developed (Map 32 a–d). They include West and East Sepik, Gulf, Southern Highlands and West New Britain districts, though with the development of the Hoskins oil palm project (Map 33) the last of these is also becoming an important focus for in-migration. In Chimbu District and Maprik sub-district, shortage of land for subsistence and commercial agriculture is an important factor causing out-migration.

Comparison of Map 8b and Maps 32 a–d and 34 clearly shows the importance of the areas of greatest non-indigenous economic activity as destinations for migrants. A counterflow occurs from more economically and socially developed districts to those of lesser development. These migrants tend to have above average education and fill higher status and salary positions in both government and private sectors. There are two major migration links of long standing between specific districts. The first is the movement from the Sepik, Madang and Morobe areas to New Britain and New Ireland, and the second is from Western and Gulf to Central District. The former movement was well established by 1914. Since 1949, movement from the Highlands to Central District and the New Guinea islands has increased rapidly while the swing from agreement to casual employment has resulted in more complex migration linkages.

Migration is both sex and age selective. The high ratio of males to females in urban areas is indicative of this, while 8·6 per cent of indigenous males are resident outside their district of birth compared with only 3·7 per cent of females. However, more migrants are now bringing wives and children from their villages to their new homes. In Port Moresby, with a large proportion of in-migrants, 42·9 per cent of the indigenous population are in the 15–29 age group, the national figure being 24·6 per cent. This causes concern about the loss of able-bodied men to agriculture in source areas, and the number of apparently unemployed men in towns.

Bibliography:

Bureau of Statistics, n.d. (1968–69). *Population Census, 1966, Preliminary Bulletins,* Port Moresby.

Brookfield, H. C., 1960. "Population Distribution and Labour Migration in New Guinea", *Australian Geographer,* Vol. 6, pp. 233–242.

Dept. of Labour, n.d. Unpublished statistics.

In the absence of compulsory birth and death registration or successive censuses it is impossible to calculate net internal migration over a uniform time period. The only comprehensive data are provided by the 1966 census in which the population of each district is classified according to district of birth. The circles in Map 8a are proportional to the number of indigenous persons who were living outside their natal district in 1966. Each circle is shaded to show what proportion these 'out-migrants' form of the total population born in their district. The size of circles in Map 8b is proportional to the number of residents in each district who were born elsewhere. The shading indicates what percentage these form of total residents. No information is available on frequency of movement between birth and the date of census. It should be noted that Chimbu District was actually formed during the census period and consequent misenumeration may account for the surprisingly high rate of in-migration shown.

Three types of migration may be recognized. Within the traditional society shifts of residence occur as villagers take up new land, or move following marriage, disputes and, formerly, warfare. These are usually short-distance moves and make up a small proportion of inter-district migration. In areas

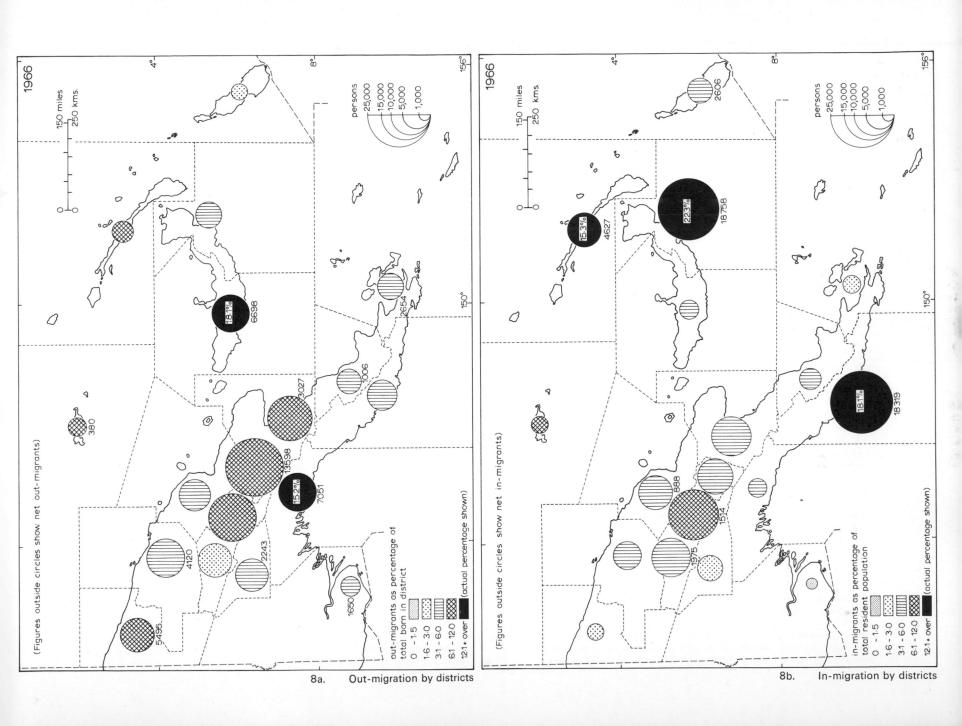

1966

150 miles
250 kms.

persons
25,000
15,000
10,000
5,000
1,000

(Figures outside circles show net out-migrants)

out-migrants as percentage of
total born in district

0 - 1.5
1.6 - 3.0
3.1 - 6.0
6.1 - 12.0
12.1+ over   (actual percentage shown)

380
5495
4120
2243
1650
13598
3027
7051   15.2%
1006
2654
6698   18.1%

8a.   Out-migration by districts

1966

150 miles
250 kms.

persons
25,000
15,000
10,000
5,000
1,000

(Figures outside circles show net in-migrants)

in-migrants as percentage of
total resident population

0 - 1.5
1.6 - 3.0
3.1 - 6.0
6.1 - 12.0
12.1+ over   (actual percentage shown)

2606
4627   15.3%
18758   22.3%
18319   18.1%
888
1514
1975

8b.   In-migration by districts

INDIGENOUS LANGUAGES

S. A. WURM *

In Papua and New Guinea, two radically different types of indigenous languages are spoken : Austronesian, and Non-Austronesian or Papuan. The Austronesian languages of the area, often referred to as Melanesian, are mostly located in coastal, near-coastal and insular regions. The Austronesian languages, which are all inter-related and number around 200 (two-thirds of which are found in the eastern insular and the extreme eastern mainland areas) are immigrant languages, and their ancestors are believed to have moved in from the west perhaps 5,000 years ago. Most are the languages of small to very small speech communities and the total number of their speakers constitutes under 15 per cent of the entire population of Papua and New Guinea. The Papuan languages occupy the bulk of the mainland portion of Papua and New Guinea, and most of the southern half of Bougainville. Only seven Papuan languages are found in the New Britain-New Ireland area. The total number of Papuan languages in Papua and New Guinea is in the vicinity of 500, and while most are spoken by small or very small speech communities, a limited number have over 10,000 speakers each, with the numerically largest language, Enga in the Western Highlands District having over 130,000 speakers.

Until only a decade or so ago, it had been thought that the Papuan languages were generally unrelated to each other—only a few smallish groups of inter-related languages had been known to exist. However, the results of intensive linguistic work during the last decade or so, and in particular during the last few years, have shown that the great majority of the Papuan languages could be included in a limited number of predominantly large to very large groups of inter-related languages, known as phyla. Most of these phyla could be sub-divided into sub-groups, called stocks, and these in turn into language families. Some of the small phyla consist of only a single stock, or a single family. Eighteen large and small phyla are located wholly or in part within the borders of Papua and New Guinea. Of these, six are very small and contain only from two to six languages, though one of these, the Toaripi Family in the Gulf District, which by itself constitutes a phylum and contains four languages, has over 30,000 speakers. Of the remaining large phyla, five (i.e. the East New

Guinea Highlands, the Finisterre-Huon, the Southeast New Guinea, the Central and South, and the Madang Phyla) have been found to be related to each other. Together with other groups in West Irian they constitute a very large super-group of inter-related Papuan languages which occupies about three-quarters of the entire island of New Guinea, and has been named the Central New Guinea Macro-Phylum. A sixth phylum, called the North Papuan Phylum, which is located almost entirely in West Irian and overlaps into Australian New Guinea only in the West Sepik District, also seems to link with the Macro-Phylum. However, the relationship of the Australian New Guinea section of it with the rest of the North Papuan Phylum, and with the Macro-Phylum is now in doubt. Three more phyla, i.e. the Middle Sepik-Upper Sepik-Sepik Hill Phylum (this may in fact constitute two or three separate phyla), the Adelbert Range Phylum, and the Anga Stock (or Family) which by itself constitutes a phylum, may perhaps also prove to be parts of the Macro-Phylum. Three other phyla in Papua and New Guinea, the Torricelli, Ramu and Bougainville Phyla, are apparently not related to the Macro-Phylum phyla. A few as yet doubtful additional groups have been reported, and about 50 languages, so-called isolates, which at present are not relatable to each other or to any of the established groups, are located in various points of the Territory. Some small parts of the Gulf, East Sepik, West Sepik and Madang Districts are still linguistically unknown.

The Austronesian languages have a comparatively simple structure, but the Papuan languages are mostly of enormous structural complexity which manifests itself especially in the verbal systems. A sometimes bewildering range of references to the number etc. of the subject, direct and indirect object, and beneficiary of an action, of tenses, aspects, moods and circumstances under which an action is performed, are indicated in the verb in some languages, and in many, special, and often intricate, forms appear with verbs which are not the final verb in a sentence. Nouns often display complex class systems, and adjectives, demonstratives, numerals, subject and object markers with verbs, etc. vary for the classes of the nouns to which they refer.

* Professor of Linguistics, Research School of Pacific Studies, Australian National University.

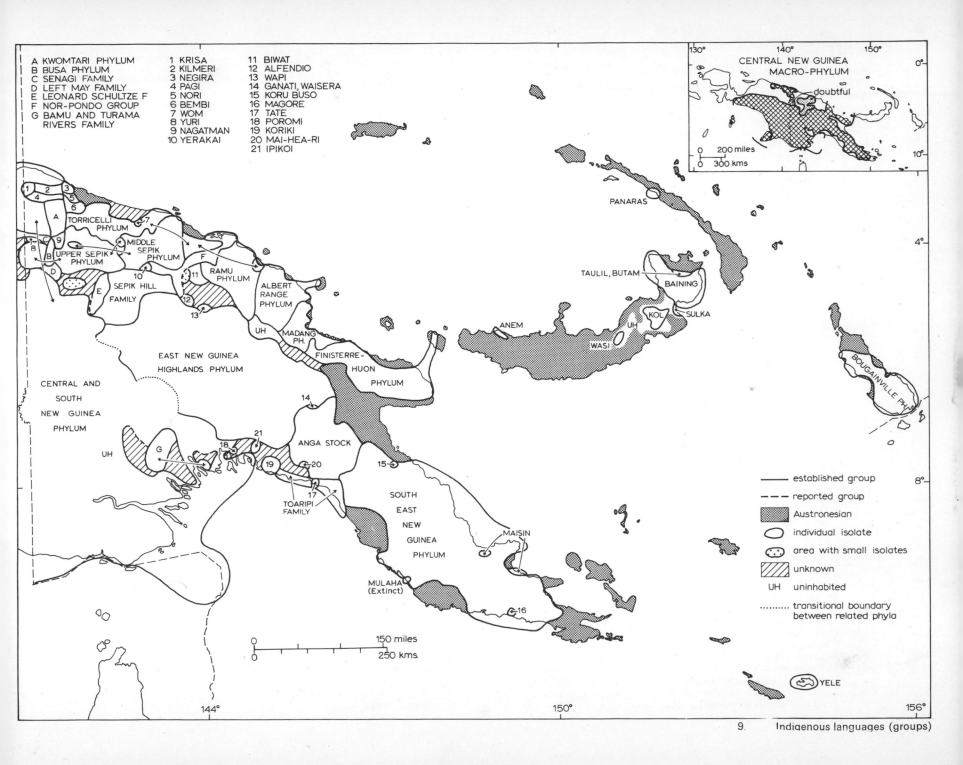

A KWOMTARI PHYLUM
B BUSA PHYLUM
C SENAGI FAMILY
D LEFT MAY FAMILY
E LEONARD SCHULTZE F
F NOR-PONDO GROUP
G BAMU AND TURAMA
  RIVERS FAMILY

1 KRISA
2 KILMERI
3 NEGIRA
4 PAGI
5 NORI
6 BEMBI
7 WOM
8 YURI
9 NAGATMAN
10 YERAKAI

11 BIWAT
12 ALFENDIO
13 WAPI
14 GANATI, WAISERA
15 KORU BUSO
16 MAGORE
17 TATE
18 POROMI
19 KORIKI
20 MAI-HEA-RI
21 IPIKOI

CENTRAL NEW GUINEA
MACRO-PHYLUM

doubtful

0   200 miles
0   300 kms

PANARAS

TAULIL, BUTAM
BAINING
ANEM
KOL
SULKA
UH
WASI
BOUGAINVILLE PH.

TORRICELLI
PHYLUM
MIDDLE
SEPIK PHYLUM
UPPER SEPIK
PHYLUM
RAMU PHYLUM
ALBERT
RANGE
PHYLUM
SEPIK HILL
FAMILY
UH
MADANG
PH.
FINISTERRE-
HUON
PHYLUM

EAST NEW GUINEA
HIGHLANDS PHYLUM

CENTRAL AND
SOUTH
NEW GUINEA
PHYLUM

UH

ANGA STOCK

G

TOARIPI
FAMILY

SOUTH
EAST
NEW
GUINEA
PHYLUM

MAISIN

MULAHA
(Extinct)

established group
reported group
Austronesian
individual isolate
area with small isolates
unknown
UH uninhabited
.... transitional boundary
between related phyla

YELE

150 miles
250 kms.

9. Indigenous languages (groups)

NOTES

Family: A group of two or more inter-related languages which, in general, share about 28 per cent or more basic vocabulary cognates.

Stock: A group of two or more inter-related families in which, in general, member languages of one of the families share between about 12 and 28 per cent basic vocabulary cognates with member languages of the other families. One, more, or all of the member families of a stock can consist of single languages each. Such languages are referred to as *family-level languages* or *family-level (language) isolates.*

Phylum: A group of two or more inter-related stocks in which, in general, member languages of one of the stocks share between about 5 to 12 per cent basic vocabulary cognates with member languages of the other stocks. One, more, or all of the stocks can consist of single families each. Such families are referred to as *stock-level families* or *stock-level family isolates.* At the same time, one, more or all of the stocks can consist of single languages each. Such languages are known as *stock-level languages* or *stock-level (language) isolates.*

Macro-phylum: A group of inter-related phyla in which, in general, member languages of one of the phyla share 5 per cent or less basic vocabulary cognates with member languages of the other phyla. One or more of the phyla can consist of a single stock, single family or single language each. These are called *phylum-level stocks, families or languages,* or *phylum-level stock, family, or language isolates.* The same term is used if such phyla are not members of a macro-phylum, and have at this stage no known relationship links with other languages. A considerable number of individual Papuan languages belong to this category, and are also known as *phylum-level isolates.*

Stocks (Including Stock-Level Families and Language Isolates)
(*indicates language in adjacent area of West Irian)

a	Sentani Family (stock-level family)*
b	Nimboran Family (stock-level family)*
c	Tami Stock
d	Sko Family (may belong to the Torricelli Phylum, not to the Central and South New Guinea Phylum, or may perhaps even be a separate phylum) (stock-level family?)
e	Fas Stock
f	Kwomtari Family (stock-level family)
g	Busa (stock-level isolate)
h	Amto (stock-level isolate)
i	West Wapei Family (stock-level family)
j	Palei Stock
k	Maimai Stock
l	an unnamed stock-level isolate
m	Valman (stock-level isolate)
n	Yapunda (stock-level isolate)
o	Bragat (stock-level isolate)
p	Eitiep (stock-level isolate)
q	Buna Stock (or stock-level family)
r	Monumbo Family (stock-level family)
s	Namie (stock-level isolate)
t	Middle Sepik Stock
u	Upper Sepik Stock
v	Ram Family (stock-level family)
w	Tama Family (stock-level family)
x	Kambot (stock-level isolate)
y	Aion (stock-level isolate)

z	Agoan Family (stock-level family)
aa	Ruboni Stock
bb	Goam Stock
cc	Annaberg Stock
dd	Josephstaal Stock
ee	Pihom Stock
ff	Isumrud Stock
gg	Wanang Stock
hh	Mugil (stock-level isolate)
ii	Mabuso Stock
jj	Astrolabe Bay Stock (composition unknown)
kk	Rai Coast Stock
ll	Finisterre Stock
mm	Huon Stock
nn	Kovai (stock-level isolate)
oo	East New Guinea Highlands Stock
pp	Foi (or Kutubu) Stock (constitutes a link between the East New Guinea Highlands Phylum and the Central and South New Guinea Phylum). It now seems that it is not an independent stock, but a part of the Central and South New Guinea Stock.
qq	Mikaru Family (stock-level family)
rr	Pawaia Family (stock-level family)
ss	Goilala Family (stock-level family)
tt	Binandere Stock
uu	Koiari-Manubara-Yareba Stock
vv	Daga Family (stock-level family)
ww	Oksapmin (stock-level isolate; it may however be a phylum-level isolate—its relationship to the Central and South New Guinea Phylum is doubtful).
xx	Central and South New Guinea Stock
yy	Marind Stock
zz	Suki-Gogodala Stock
ab	Yey-Kanum-Moraori Stock
ac	Morehead River Stock
ad	Agöb Family (stock-level family). This family shows quite strong lexical links with ac and af, and it may perhaps be possible to combine the three into a single stock.
ae	Tirio Family (stock-level family)
af	Oriomo River Family (stock-level family)
ag	Kiwai Family (stock-level family)
ah	Miriam (stock-level isolate)
ai	Kikori River Family (stock-level family)
aj	Kunua-Keriaka-Rotokas-Eivo Stock
ak	Nasioi-Nagovisi-Siwai-Buin Stock

Families (and Family-level Language Isolates)

1–21	See map 9
22	Upper Tami famili(es)?*
23	Arso Family*
24	Skofro Family
25	Waris Family
26	Fas (family-level isolate)
27	Baibai (family-level isolate)
28	Wapei Family
29	Palei Family

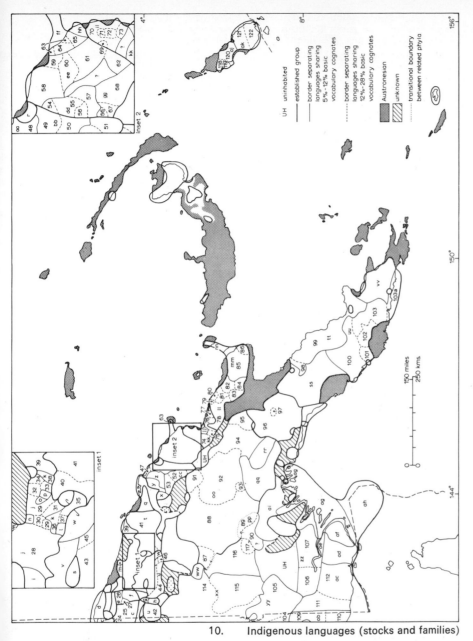

10. Indigenous languages (stocks and families)

UH uninhabited
— established group
— border separating languages sharing 5%-12% basic vocabulary cognates
---- border separating languages sharing 12%-28% basic vocabulary cognates
Austronesian
unknown
transitional boundary between related phyla

30 Agi (family-level isolate)
31 Kayik (family-level isolate)
32 Lou Family
33 Kalp (family-level isolate)
34 Yambes (family-level isolate)
35 Maimai Family
36 Wiaki (family-level isolate)
37 Beli (family-level isolate)
38 Urat (family-level isolate)
39 Arapesh Family
40 Kwoma Family
41 Ndu Family
42 Abau (family-level isolate)
43 Amal (family-level isolate)
44 Iwam (family-level isolate)
70 Hanseman Family
71 Nake (family-level isolate)
72 Gal (family-level isolate)
73 Abaian Family
74 Urisino Family
75 Evapia Family
76 Kabenau Family
77 Yaganon Family
78 Gusap-Mot Family
79 Dahating (family-level isolate)
80 Warup Family
81 Yupna Family
82 Uruwa Family
83 Wantoat Family
84 Erap Family
85 Western Huon Family
86 Eastern Huon Family
87 Duna (family-level isolate)
88 West-Central Family
89 Foi (or Kutubu) (family-level isolate)
90 Fasu (family-level isolate)
91 Karam Family
92 Central Family
93 Wiru (family-level isolate)·
94 East-Central Family
95 Eastern Family
96 Kapau-Menye Family
97 Langimar (family-level isolate)
98 Guhu Samane (family-level isolate)
99 Binandere Family
100 Koiari Family
101 Kwale (family-level isolate)
102 Manubara Family
103 Yareba Family } probably constituting a single family
103a Mailu Family
104 Central Marind Family
105 Eastern Marind Family
106 Suki (family-level isolate)
107 Gogodala Family
108 Moraori (family-level isolate) *
109 Yey (family-level isolate)

110 Kanum (family-level isolate)
111 Bensbach Family
112 Morehead-Mai Kussa Family
113 Awyu Family*
114 Ok Family
115 Awin-Pare Family
116 Samo-Beami Family
117 Bosavi (family-level isolate)
118 Kunua (family-level isolate)
119 Keriaka (family-level isolate)
120 Rotokas Family
121 Nasioi Family
122 Buin Family

LINGUE FRANCHE

S. A. WURM

The multiplicity and diversity of languages in Papua and New Guinea has, almost from the beginning of European contact (and in one instance before), encouraged the development and use of lingue franche for communication beyond the mostly very narrow confines of a particular local language. The currency of most of these lingue franche is geographically quite restricted, and several of the smaller ones have been rapidly losing ground to Pidgin and English in recent years.

With the exception of the two major lingue franche, Police Motu and Pidgin, the lingue franche owe their role to missions who adopted them for use as church languages, and for general missionary activities.

Kâte, a Papuan language originally spoken by a few hundred people in the Finschhafen area was adopted as a mission language by the Lutheran Mission about 1900 and has become the regional lingua franca of the Huon Peninsula area. It has also been introduced into the Highlands. Estimated to be spoken and understood by about 60,000 people, its currency has spread beyond the missionary sphere, at least in parts of the Huon Peninsula.

Yabêm, originally a numerically insignificant Austronesian language spoken in the southeast of Huon Peninsula, was also adopted by the Lutheran Mission, mainly for use in Austronesian-speaking areas. Today it is spoken and understood by many thousands in coastal and riverine parts of the Morobe District.

Gedaged (Graged) or Bel, an Austronesian language, was adopted by the Lutheran Mission as a more restricted regional lingua franca for use in some coastal and insular areas of Madang District.

Tolai (or Kuanua), a numerically strong Austronesian language in northern New Britain, was adopted by both Catholics and Methodists for use in the New Britain-New Ireland area.

Wedau, an Austronesian language, has been used by the Anglicans in much of the coastal part of the mainland portion of Milne Bay District, and its currency extends into Northern District.

Dobu, an Austronesian language, was adopted by the Methodist Mission for use in some insular parts of Milne Bay District.

Suau, an Austronesian language, was adopted by the Kwato Mission for use in southern coastal parts of Milne Bay District. Its currency extends into the adjacent parts of Central District.

Motu proper, the numerically strong Austronesian language of the Port Moresby area, was adopted by the London Missionary Society for use in the Port Moresby area and in some adjacent Austronesian-speaking areas.

Toaripi, a numerically strong coastal Papuan language in the eastern part of Gulf District, has been used by the London Missionary Society and the Catholics in that area.

(Island) Kiwai, a Papuan language spoken on Kiwai Island in the Fly estuary, has been used by the London Missionary Society in coastal areas of the Western District. Its currency extends beyond the missionary sphere, though as a secular regional lingua franca, it is giving way to Coastal Kiwai, a closely related language spoken in southeastern coastal parts of Western District.

Of the two major lingue franche of the Territory, Police Motu, came into being in pre-European times as a trade language used by the Motu of the Port Moresby area during their annual trading expeditions to the Papuan Gulf region. It was a pidginized Motu, and was later adopted for general use by the Royal Papuan Constabulary—hence its name. It is today spoken by 120,000 indigenes of 10 years of age and over in many parts of Papua, but is now rapidly losing ground to Pidgin.

Pidgin is a daughter language of Beach-la-Mar, the English-based South Sea pidgin language of the early 19th century. Beach-la-Mar developed from Chinese pidgin English which is believed to have originated from the English relexification of an earlier Portuguese-based pidgin used in Chinese ports. Pidgin came into being in its ancestral form on the sugar-cane plantations of North Queensland in the mid-19th century, as an inter-native lingua franca, used by indentured labourers from Melanesia. It spread back into Melanesia, and the form used in Rabaul, the German administrative capital, around 1900 spread rapidly through many parts of German New Guinea. This spread accelerated after the Australian take-over in 1914. It is, and always has been, primarily an inter-native lingua franca, and is moving towards universality in the Territory. It is at present spoken by 530,000 indigenes of 10 years of age and over, but this figure is increasing very rapidly, and Pidgin is advancing into several parts of Papua at the expense of Police Motu. There are indications that it may become the future national language of the emerging nation, side by side with English (at present spoken by almost 200,000 indigenes of 10 years of age and over) as the official language.

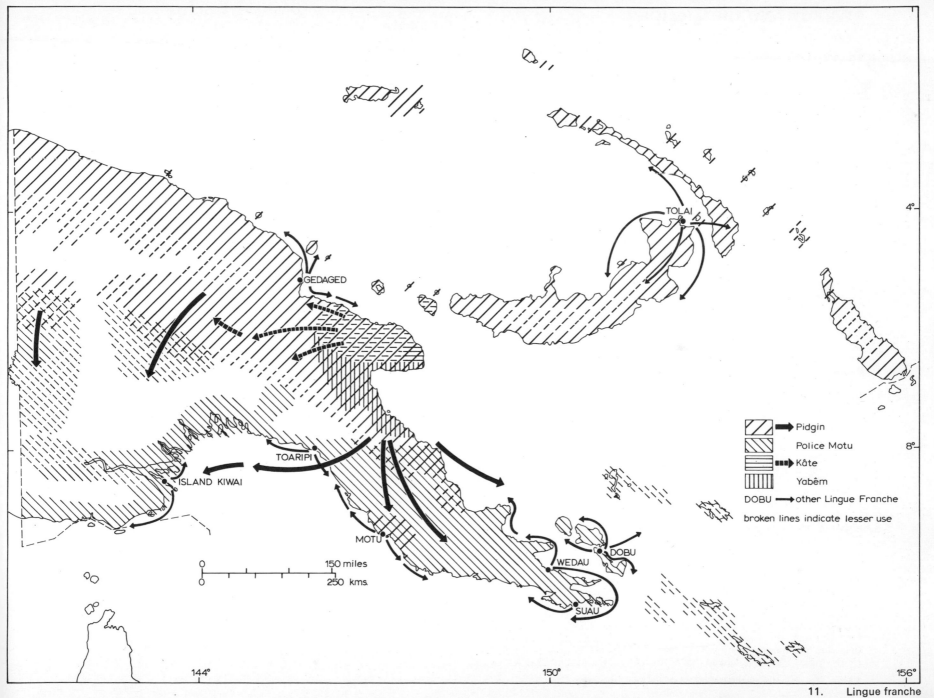

TOLAI

GEDAGED

TOARIPI

ISLAND KIWAI

MOTU

WEDAU

DOBU

SUAU

▨ ➤	Pidgin
▨ ➤	Police Motu
▤ ➤	Kâte
▥	Yabêm
DOBU ➤	other Lingue Franche

broken lines indicate lesser use

0   150 miles

0   250 kms.

4°

8°

144°

150°

156°

11.   Lingue franche

RELIGION AND THE MISSIONS

D. J. DICKSON *

The nineteenth century missionary enterprise reached New Guinea at a time when the enterprise itself was at its strongest and most universal but when its base support in church-going people in the homelands was being eroded by secularism. The Missions were primarily evangelical; they presented a simplified evangel to meet the needs of an unsophisticated people and a multiplicity of languages; and they did this while the non-missionary contact was becoming increasingly secular and increasingly sophisticated. Thus the confusion of the clash of native and western cultures was compounded by a dualism in the value, belief and behaviour patterns brought by the missionaries and the frequently different patterns of western secular society. Confronted with this, and other, problems, the tendency of the Missions was, until recently, to guard against the inroads of secular society rather than to be agents of it. The work of the Missions in translation, education and, to a degree, even medicine, was designed to win Christian adherents. The first translations were invariably Bible extracts, hymns, church history and the lives of saints. Training schools were established for priests, pastors, catechists and evangelists and the trained village pastor/teacher combined his roles with little modification on all days of the week. Medical assistance and evangelism both were the responsibility of the nursing sisters and doctors and their trainees. The Missions tended to permeate the whole life of the village with their message and its expected behaviour patterns. In all these activities the missionary purpose was primarily the creation of Christian communities, not the re-building of village life. Missionary attitudes varied from authoritarian to paternalistic and the positive response, at least superficially, from acquiescence to obedience. There was some opposition and many missionaries became martyrs in the early days of contact, and many succumbed to disease.

The areas of Missions influence tended to be clearly defined in the pre-war period and a brief account of their origin is useful, as a comparison of Map 12 with Map 13 will show how the early pattern of establishment is still apparent in the present distribution of religious adherence. The pattern for Papua was determined at a meeting of London Missionary Society (L.M.S.), Anglican and Methodist missionaries in 1890. Such a spheres-of-influence policy could not withstand the pressures for expansion of the Catholic Mission or the demands for entry of new missions. By the 1930s the Mission of the Sacred Heart (M.S.C.) area overlapped that of the L.M.S.; the Seventh Day Adventist

* Senior Lecturer in History, University of Papua and New Guinea.

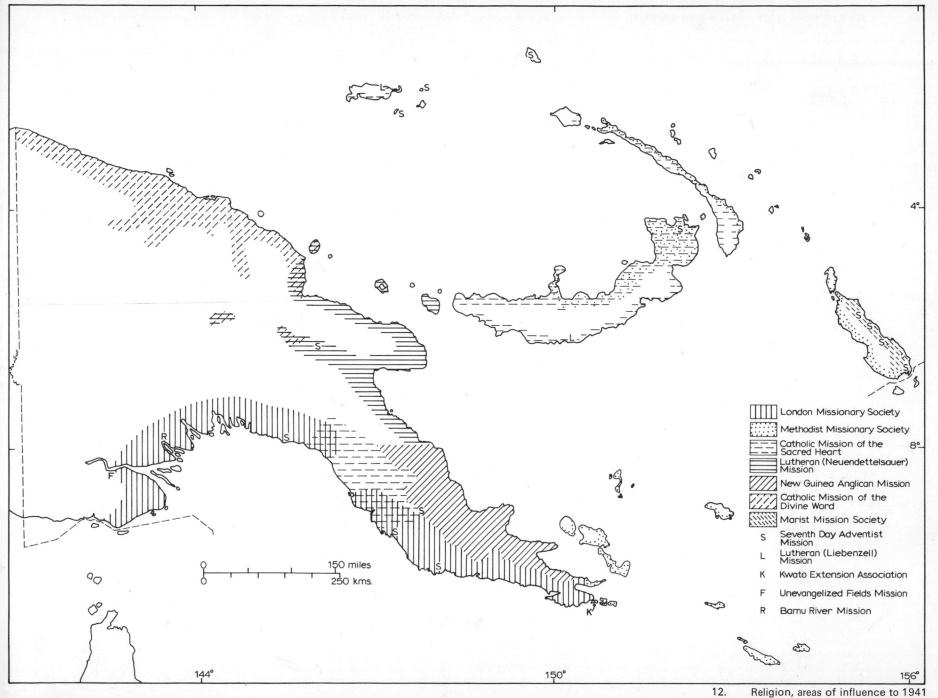

London Missionary Society	
Methodist Missionary Society	
Catholic Mission of the Sacred Heart	
Lutheran (Neuendettelsauer) Mission	
New Guinea Anglican Mission	
Catholic Mission of the Divine Word	
Marist Mission Society	
S	Seventh Day Adventist Mission
L	Lutheran (Liebenzell) Mission
K	Kwato Extension Association
F	Unevangelized Fields Mission
R	Bamu River Mission

150 miles

250 kms.

12.   Religion, areas of influence to 1941

(S.D.A.) Mission had begun at Bisianumu in 1908 and extended to five other stations, and the Bamu River Mission and the Unevangelised Fields Mission had begun work. A spheres-of-influence policy was also attempted under German Administration in New Britain from 1890 to 1899. The northeast portion of the Gazelle Peninsula was reserved for the Methodist Mission while the M.S.C., which had arrived seven years later, was expected to work south of this area. Catholic pressure and the impracticability of the policy forced its abandonment. Catholic and Methodist influence in New Britain and New Ireland were affected only by the coming of the Seventh Day Adventists (S.D.A.) to the Rabaul area and the St. Matthias Group, and the small Lutheran station opened near Gasmata. No spheres of influence policy was imposed on mainland New Guinea or on Bougainville. In New Guinea, Catholic and Lutheran areas were adjacent or overlapping in some areas and in 1934 the S.D.A. began at Kainantu. On Bougainville, Methodists and the Marist Mission Society were mainly on the southwest and northeast coasts respectively, with some intermingling, while the S.D.A. established stations on the east coast in the 1930s. It is probable that neither the presence nor absence of spheres-of-influence policies was the determining factor in relations between Missions, which could be described more aptly as absence of conflict than presence of co-operation. Each Mission could find, without encroaching on another's territory, thousands of souls to be saved, bodies to be healed, minds to be educated, and people to be assisted to a new way of life according to the codes of western Christian society. Any sectarian antipathies held by missionaries became relatively unwanted equipment among the skills and materials necessary for such basic needs as roads, bridges, schools, hospitals, and above all, a language to communicate the gospel.

The catastrophe of war permanently altered the missionary scene. Almost all Missions suffered the loss of missionaries killed, buildings and equipment destroyed and plantations razed. In the re-building several significant changes occurred. Missions' expenditures very greatly increased and have been matched by increased Government aid attracted by medical and educational services. In 1966 the Missions spent from their own funds $3,558,000 and an additional $2,142,000 from grants-in-aid. Expenditure on education has been about three times that on health. Another change of importance is the growth in numbers of Missions operating. There are now 33 Missions (pre-war, 6), if we omit the sub-divisions of religious groups holding the same doctrinal position. If we include the latter (e.g., in the Catholic Missions, the orders M.S.C., Society of the Divine Word (S.V.D.), Marist, Capuchin, Franciscan, Montford, Marianhill) there are now 52 Missions (pre-war, 12). Specialist inter-denominational agencies add to diversity: for example, the Missionary Aviation Fellowship, the Christian Radio Missionary Fellowship, the British and Foreign Bible Society, Campaigners for Christ, and others. There is a corresponding growth in numbers of missionaries (1966: 3,246) a high proportion of whom (38 per cent) come from the United States or continental Europe. A positive gain of the diversification of Catholic and Protestant effort is the greater area covered and number of people responding to the Christian evangel and its social development corollaries. A comparison of the areas of Christian influence in 1966 with those of 1941 is a clear indication of this. Available statistics make the same point. It is emphasised that Map 13 and the statistics on adherents following (and those appearing in missionary sources which may be compared with them) must be interpreted in the light of the differences among denominations and administration officers in their definitions of "adherent" and other classifications, e.g., "communicant", "member", "catechumen", and others. Taking "adherents" to mean whatever degree of commitment to the Christian religion is understood by those supplying the figures, the 1966 Census returns for the eight largest Missions are (rounded, with proportion of total adherents in brackets) Catholic, 672,000 (34 per cent); Lutheran, 594,000 (30 per cent); Methodist, 183,000 (9 per cent); Papua Ekalesia, 130,000 (7 per cent); Evangelical Alliance, 115,000 (6 per cent); Anglican, 104,000 (5 per cent); Adventist, 71,000 (4 per cent); Baptist, 45,000 (2 per cent). Total adherents claimed are 1,984,201, or 92 per cent of total population.

In spite of the immediate post-war diversification there has grown a degree of ecumenicism not yet achieved in metropolitan countries. A Melanesian Council of Churches includes all the large and some of the small (in Australian terms) Protestant denominations and there is hope that Catholic representation will be added. A more fundamentalist grouping is in the Evangelical Alliance but one denomination (Baptist) is a member of both organizations. Meetings of the Ministers Fraternal include representation from Catholic, Lutheran and most Protestant bodies and a Melanesian Association of Theological Schools includes most denominations. To a large degree the competitive element in proselytism has been replaced by co-operation. But some fundamentalist groups have not joined the Evangelical Alliance; most in the Alliance could not support the Melanesian Council of Churches, and some sects, for example, the Adventists and the Jehovah's Witnesses, maintain a consistently separatist evangelistic and training policy. In some ways related to ecumenicism has been the change from "Mission" to "Church". Lutheran groups amalgamated in 1953 and formed an indigenous Lutheran Church (ELCONG) in 1956 with the plan of "lateral withdrawal" of all expatriates as indigenous leadership became possible in specialist medical and educational fields. The L.M.S. handed over control to the indigenous Papua Ekalesia in 1962. The Methodist Missions joined them to form the United Church in early 1968. The Anglican Church became independent in 1969 and indigenous control may be expected to develop.

The three major emphases of the pre-war and immediate post-war years were evangelism, education and health services. The last decade has seen the development of a fourth, socio-economic services. Some elements of this could be seen in the large pre-war plantations and other commercial operations in M.S.C., S.V.D. and Lutheran areas, but now the emphasis is not only upon providing a financial base for an independent church but also upon assisting the general socio-economic advancement of the people; for example, in the Mendi tea plantations developed by the Capuchin Mission, and the Lutheran co-operative Native Marketing and Supply (NAMASU). Missionaries are also operating as agents or unofficial "extension officers" of Government departments and instrumentalities in such ventures as the formation of Co-operatives, Savings and Loan Societies, and the development of scientific agriculture. This is an interesting phenomenon. In metropolitan countries the nineteenth and twentieth centuries have seen secular institutions taking over the social functions of religion. In New Guinea the secular administration, conscious of the quickening pace of emergent nationalism and aware of the degree of commitment and specialized skills available in Missions and Churches, has embraced the idea of partnership in the socio-economic enterprise. For the Missions and Churches the evangel is still pre-eminent, but ecumenicism, local autonomy and socio-economic activity have taken the place of former exclusiveness and narrowness and are forging more comprehensive links with the people.

Bibliography:
Australian Council of Churches, 1965. *Responsibility in New Guinea,* Report of an Australian Ecumenical Visit to Papua and New Guinea.
Encyclopedia of the Lutheran Church, 1965. Augsburg Publishing House.
New Catholic Encyclopedia, 1967. McGraw Hill, N.Y.
Seventh Day Adventist Encyclopedia, 1966. Washington, D.C.

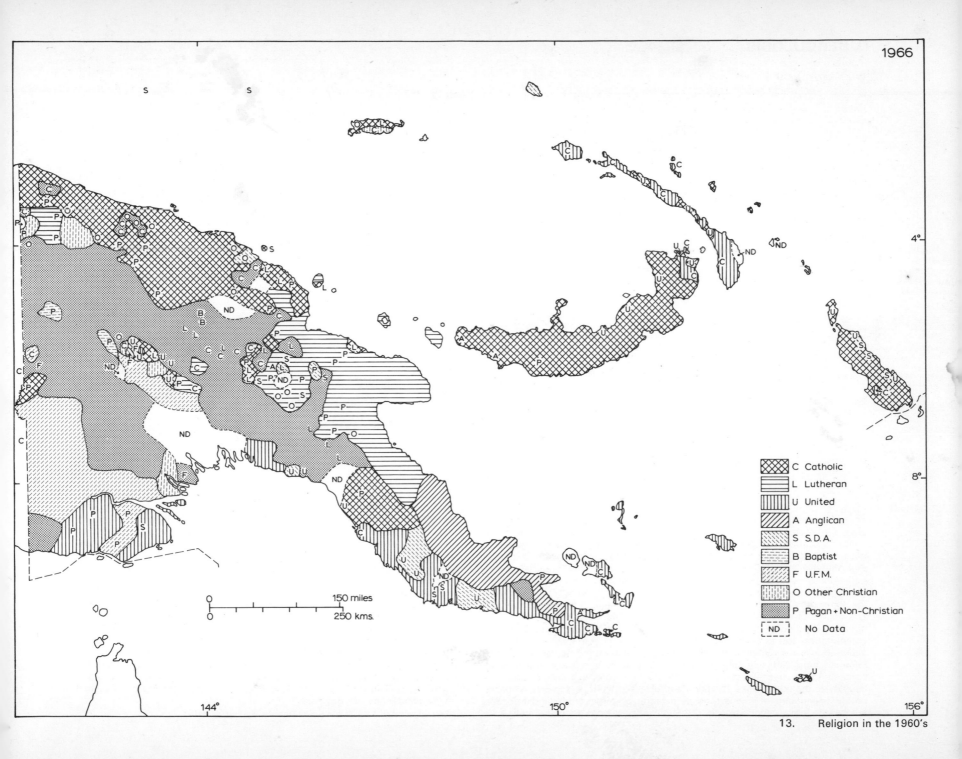

1966

C	Catholic
L	Lutheran
U	United
A	Anglican
S	S.D.A.
B	Baptist
F	U.F.M.
O	Other Christian
P	Pagan + Non-Christian
ND	No Data

150 miles

250 kms.

144° 150° 156°

4°

8°

13. Religion in the 1960's

TUBERCULOSIS

S. C. WIGLEY *

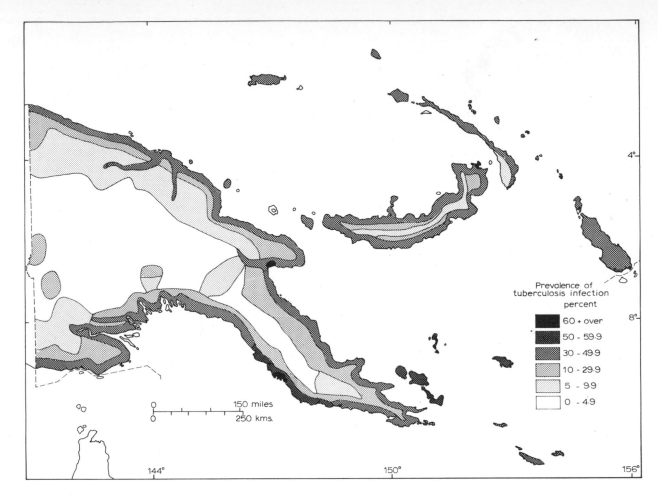

Prevalence of
tuberculosis infection
percent

■	60 + over
■	50 - 59·9
▨	30 - 49·9
▦	10 - 29·9
░	5 - 9·9
□	0 - 4·9

0 ___ 150 miles
0 ___ 250 kms.

The proper antiquity of tuberculosis in New Guinea is not known, but it is likely that it was here before the advent of European settlement and development. Widespread dissemination of the disease was impossible, however, because of the traditional life-style of the Melanesian, and it can be assumed that the disease was well contained, if not eliminated altogether, in the communities. Over the greater part of the past century other influences, largely connected with the development of the country, have been operating to define the immediate picture of tuberculosis amongst the indigenous population. The degree of tuberculous infection amongst Papuans and New Guineans is directly proportional to the degree and duration of contact with European communities, and to the degree of urbanization or culture change which has occurred in the indigenous communities. As urbanization increases infection becomes more diffusely spread in the communities. In isolated and recently contacted rural areas infection is restricted to the older age groups, and particularly to the adult males. Infection and disease therefore is largely a coastal problem, and one of towns. The association of urbanization and infection reaches its logical conclusion in the Highlands, where vast communities are free from the disease. If the geography of a particular area, its trading patterns, and the amount of contact between the people and the heavily infected coastal areas are known, the infection rate of the particular area can be predicted very accurately.

There have been some spectacular examples of the effects of contact and urbanization on lightly tuberculinized groups of indigenes in the past. In the Goroka community two years of contact with an apparently healthy group of coastal workers raised the infection rates of Highlanders some 40 times over that of Highlanders who had not had such contact. In the Bem Island community such contact was sufficient, over one year, to increase infection rates from 10 to over 80 per cent. A 1959 study of the Manus community (which had been subjected acutely to the most malignant urbanizing influence, namely war) showed a dramatic rise in infection rates in those sections of the community which underwent this experience, in the age groups 15 years and older. This was an experience which was repeated also in the Northern District on the coast in the Oro Bay area.

* Senior Specialist (T.B.), Public Health Department, Port Moresby.

FILARIASIS

B. McMILLAN *

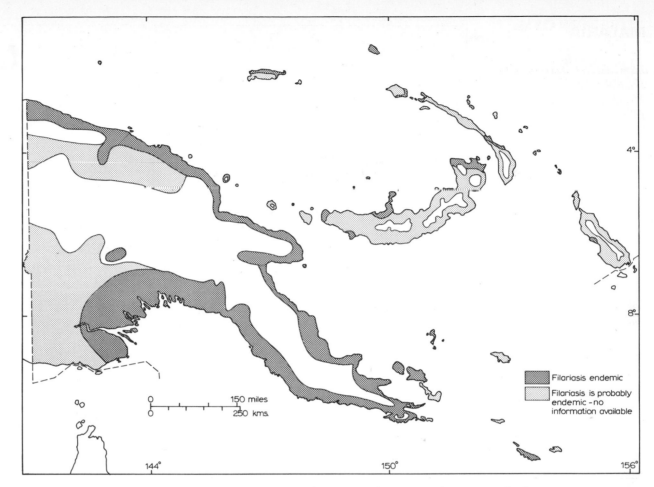

Filariasis endemic

Filariasis is probably endemic - no information available

150 miles
250 kms.

Nocturnal periodic Bancroftian filariasis is endemic in rural Papua and New Guinea up to an altitude of approximately 2,000 ft. Beyond that level it may be focally endemic depending on availability of vector breeding sites and their proximity to villages. Transmission to 4,000 ft. has been demonstrated. Subperiodic *Wuchereria bancrofti* and *Brugia malayi* have not been recorded and records of other filarial parasites of man are probably erroneous.

Within the area of distribution, there are two basic epidemiological patterns. The first is a moderate prevalence of infection associated with a low level of chronic clinical manifestations. In such villages the microfilaraemic rate may reach 30 per cent but is of low density. Elephantiasis, and hydrocele in males, may occur to the extent of one to two per cent and five per cent respectively. This pattern, which is dependent on seasonal transmission, is generally applicable throughout the Territory. The second pattern is where hyperendemic foci are found within the general area of distribution. Here the microfilaraemic rate may be over 45 per cent and of high density. Elephantiasis may be of the order of 10–15 per cent and hydrocele in males, 15 per cent. These foci are dependent on perennial transmission, this being determined by factors such as

prevailing winds, vegetation cover and even type of soil.

The prime vectors of filariasis are members of the *Anopheles punctulatus* complex (*An. punctulatus, An. farauti, An. koliensis*) which are also the most important vectors of malaria. *Mansonia uniformis,* considered an important vector in Irian Barat by Dutch workers, has not been incriminated in the Territory. Several other species of mosquitoes have been shown to be vectors of secondary importance. Although *Culex pipiens fatigans,* a domestic species, is not a good vector, increasing urbanization may result in increased transmission in towns.

Prevention of the disease depends on the individual avoiding exposure to infected mosquito bites, whereas mass control of filariasis is dependent upon the exhibition of the filaricidal drug diethylcarbamazine, preferably in conjunction with residual insecticidal spraying.

In the past, no stigma has been attached to the clinical manifestations of filariasis at village level. Education and competition, however, may change the communities' attitude to this disease.

* Senior Lecturer in Medical Parasitology, School of Public Health and Tropical Medicine, University of Sydney.

MALARIA

MALARIA BRANCH,
DEPARTMENT OF
PUBLIC HEALTH,
PORT MORESBY

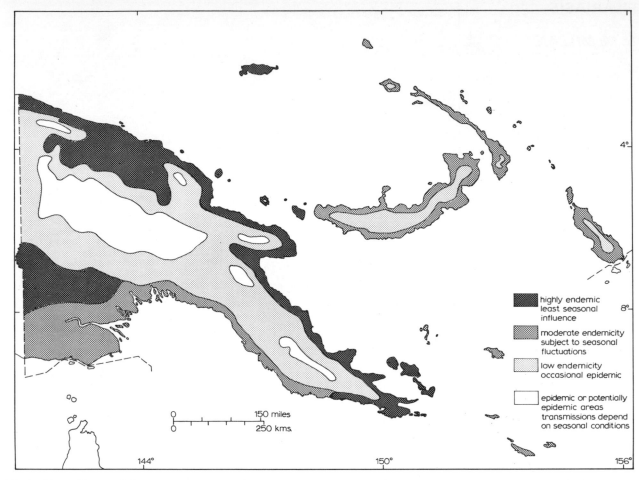

highly endemic
least seasonal
influence

moderate endemicity
subject to seasonal
fluctuations

low endemicity
occasional epidemic

epidemic or potentially
epidemic areas
transmissions depend
on seasonal conditions

150 miles
250 kms.

Malaria is the greatest single public health problem and the most important cause of ill-health in New Guinea because everywhere below 8,000 feet (2,500 metres) is potentially malarious. An estimated two-thirds of the population live in areas where the disease is endemic and the lowlands, particularly near the coast, are the areas of highest endemicity. In the highland valleys malaria has been seasonally epidemic in some years and there is evidence that the spread of malaria from the lowlands to the highlands is a by-product of European contact and economic development.

The estimation of accurate incidence and prevalence of malaria at present-day levels is rather difficult but sufficient knowledge is available to give a good picture of endemicity prior to the introduction of extensive malaria control measures. The pattern of endemicity consists of areas with varying degrees of the following:

High Endemicity: areas where innoculation is high and the continuing immunity state is high. Malaria is not obvious as a cause of illness but surveys reveal the rate to be high or constant in young children and low in adults.

Moderate Endemicity: areas where intermittent innoculation occurs resulting in occasional illnesses of adults and occasional severe manifestations among children. Surveys reveal a variable pattern, depending upon when they were done, but if parasitaemia were at a high rate in children, one would expect a moderate incidence among adults also.

Low Endemicity: areas where innoculation occurs only once a year, or perhaps only once every two or three years, resulting in severe manifestations among children and moderate morbidity among adults.

Epidemic or Potentially Epidemic Areas: areas populated by people who are generally non-immune.

The method used for the determination of the pattern of endemicity was based not only on the spleen rates alone but in some parts of the territory on the innoculation rate and the absolute parasite rate. The chief vectors of malaria transmission in Papua and New Guinea are three members of the *Anopheles punctulatus* complex: *A punctulatus A. farauti* and *A. koliensis*. Three species of human malaria are known to exist: *Plasmodium malariae, P. falciparum* and *P. vivax*. The last has a tendency to predominate in the high valleys and the first mentioned is more prevalent in the lowlands.

INTRODUCTION TO PHYSICAL ENVIRONMENT

*M. J. F. BROWN * and C. F. PAIN ***

The 10 maps in this section illustrate the salient features of the physical environment. The first two maps show how high mountain ranges form the backbone of New Guinea and associated islands. The Central Cordillera includes a complex system of ranges, generally over 12,000 ft. high, separated in many cases by broad strike valleys. The drainage pattern is extremely complex, much of it structurally controlled. There are several very large rivers, of which the Sepik, Ramu, Fly and Purari are outstanding.

New Guinea occupies a key position in the Southwest Pacific, located on the margin between the stable Australian continent and the unstable Pacific Border. Western Papua is underlain by a stable granitic basement which dips northward beneath a thin cover of Late Tertiary sediments and Alluvium. It is probably a continuation of the folded geosynclinal zone of eastern Australia (Glaessner, 1950: 858). The mountain chain of central New Guinea is not directly connected with other folded zones of the Indo-Pacific region. It expresses a large geanticline formed on the northern edge of the Australian continent.

Northern and eastern Papua and New Guinea form part of the Melanesian structural belt, which comprises the volcanic arc of the Bismarck Sea, the Morobe arc and the Owen Stanley folded zone, New Ireland and Bougainville. The area is characterized by a prevalence of sigmoidal structural trends, volcanic and seismic activity, and deep ocean trenches. The Bismarck volcanic arc is the only typical 'inner' arc in the New Guinea area and is comparable with those of Indonesia. Seismic activity is important, but, as is typical with Melanesian structures, there is a complex distribution of earthquake epicentres. The New Britain Trench, located off the southern side of the island, reaches a depth of 30,000 ft., and is continued by similar ocean deeps off the Solomons and New Hebrides.

The varied and complex landforms of Papua and New Guinea, illustrated in Map 22, are closely related to the structure and geology. The dominance of high fold mountains, with strike valleys and prominent fault scarps intensely dissected, is witness to relatively recent uplift. The steep eastern margin of the Owen Stanleys which clearly expresses the Owen Stanley Fault, the Sepik-Ramu-Markham fault trench, raised coral reefs and drowned littorals, and the prevalence of volcanic landforms, are all evidence of the geological instability of much of this region.

The final four maps show the distribution of soils, rainfall and vegetation, the characteristics of which are broadly related to the physiographic background. The effect of altitudinal range on the distribution of other physical phenomena varies a great deal, but generally leads to a vertical zonation. This is most noticeable in forest vegetation, with a sequence from lowland forest through lower montane to montane forest. Above this level (9,000–10,000 ft.) are alpine grass and herb fields. Vegetation types other than forest may be attributed to burning and shifting cultivation followed by regrowth of grasslands or savanna, and to soil and drainage conditions leading to swamp vegetation. The distribution of the major grasslands reflects to a limited extent the areas of low rainfall; that is, in the Highland valleys and the Sepik and Markham valleys.

Climate, parent material and drainage conditions are among the most important soil-forming factors. Climatic effects are mainly noticeable in the Podzol, Podzolic, Latosol, and Alpine soil groups. Drainage conditions produce hydromorphic variants of the main soil types, as well as Bog Soils associated with swamp vegetation. Parent material is important in soils such as Andosols, derived from volcanic ash, and Rendzinas, from Limestone, while Regosolic Brown Soils, Lithosols, and Alluvial Soils are more dependent on geomorphic conditions.

Bibliography

Glaessner, M. F., 1950. Geotectonic position of New Guinea, *Bull. Amer. Assoc' Petrol. Geol.* Vol. 34, pp. 856–881.

* Lecturer and ** Senior Tutor, Department of Geography, University of Papua and New Guinea.

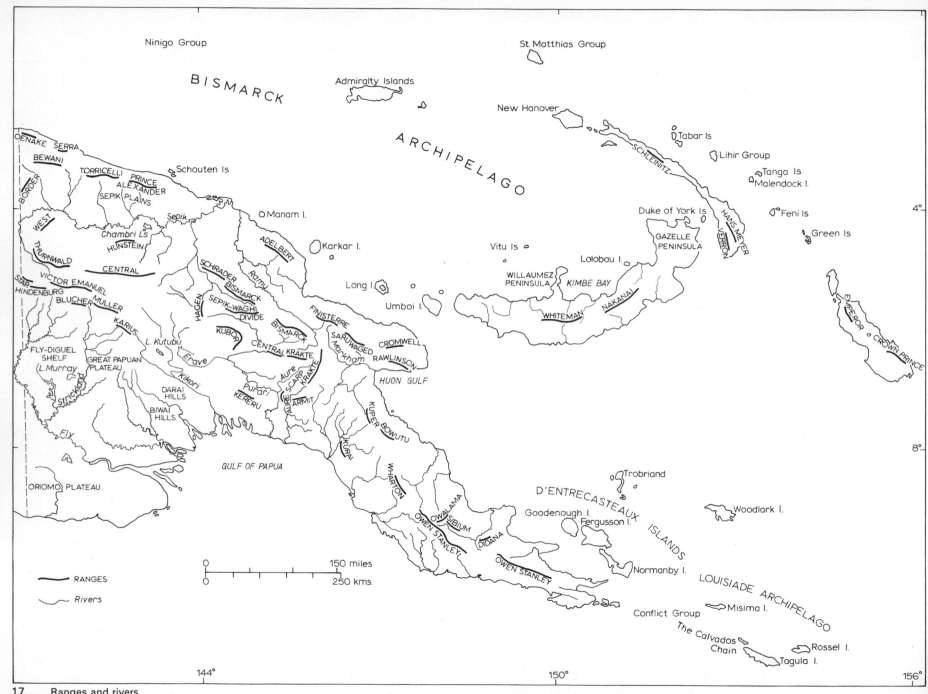

Ninigo Group

St. Matthias Group

BISMARCK

Admiralty Islands

ARCHIPELAGO

New Hanover

SCHLEINITZ

Tabar Is

Lihir Group

OENAKE SERRA

BEWANI

Schouten Is

Tanga Is

TORRICELLI PRINCE
ALEXANDER

SEPIK PLAINS

Malendock I.

BORDER

Sepik

Duke of York Is

GAZELLE
PENINSULA

HANS MEYER

VERRON

Feni Is

4°

WEST

Manam I.

Green Is

Chambri LS

HUNSTEIN

THURNWALD

CENTRAL

ADELBERT

Karkar I.

Vitu Is

Lolobau I.

VICTOR EMANUEL

SCHRADER

Ramu

Long I.

WILLAUMEZ
PENINSULA

KIMBE BAY

STAR
HINDENBURG

BLUCHER MULLER

BISMARCK

SEPIK-WAGHI
DIVIDE

HAGEN

FINISTERRE

Umboi I.

WHITEMAN

NAKANAI

EMPEROR CROWN PRINCE

KARIUS

L. Kutubu

KUBOR

BISMARCK

CENTRAL KRAKTE

SARUWAGED

CROMWELL

RAWLINSON

FLY-DIGUEL
SHELF

GREAT PAPUAN
PLATEAU

Erave

Markham

(L. Murray)

Kikori

Aure

SCARP

KRAKTE

ARMIT

HUON GULF

DARAI
HILLS

Purari

KERERU

Strickland

BIWAI
HILLS

KUPER

BOWUTU

Fly

IKURAI

GULF OF PAPUA

WHARTON

8°

ORIOMO PLATEAU

Trobriand

D'ENTRECASTEAUX ISLANDS

Woodlark I.

OWALAMA

SIBIUM

Goodenough I.

Fergusson I.

OWEN
STANLEY

DIDANA

Normanby I.

LOUISIADE ARCHIPELAGO

RANGES

150 miles

Rivers

0

250 kms.

Misima I.

Conflict Group

The Calvados
Chain

Rossel I.

Tagula I.

144°

150°

156°

17.   Ranges and rivers

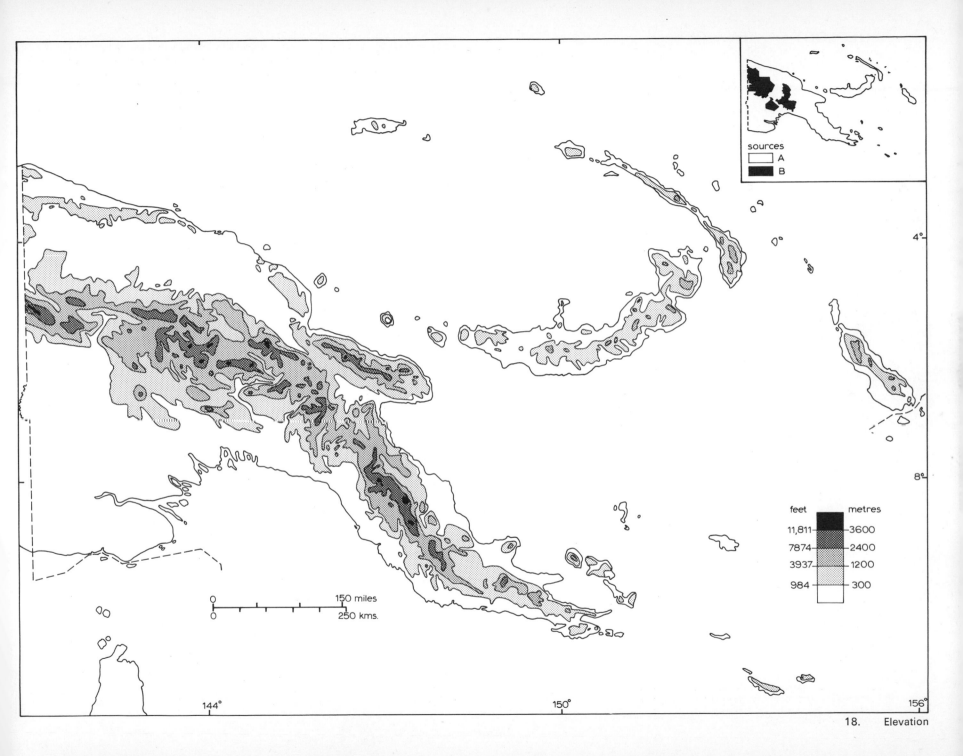

sources
A
B

feet | metres
11,811 — 3600
7874 — 2400
3937 — 1200
984 — 300

150 miles
250 kms.

4°

8°

144°

150°

156°

18.　Elevation

GEOLOGY *A. RENWICK* *

Geologic mapping in the Territory of Papua and New Guinea has been undertaken by a number of workers, principally during the present century. Reconnaissance mapping is not necessarily productive of immediate economic benefit and is for this reason normally regarded as a function of Government. Up to the time of the Second World War, the Territory of New Guinea had received more attention from Government than had Papua and, even after the two territories had been joined administratively, government sponsored work was concentrated primarily in New Guinea while the search for oil has largely dominated geologic exploration in Papua. Latterly, a systematic governmental mapping programme for the whole Territory has resulted in a more even distribution of effort, although the disparate objectives of oil exploration and general geologic mapping have resulted in some currently unresolved problems of presentation. Recognition of this fact implies no criticism of either government or company policy, but is essential to an understanding of the present state of reconnaissance geologic mapping of the Territory.

Palaeozoic

Upper Palaeozoic metamorphic rocks, exposed in eastern New Guinea, are the oldest so far discovered in the Territory. They, together with Lower Triassic granitic intrusives, form the basement for Mesozoic sedimentation in the area. Permian granite occurs in Torres Strait and has been recorded in drillholes in the Papuan Coastal Plain.

Mesozoic

In Mesozoic times, extensive geosynclinal deposition occurred in Eastern Papua, and the resulting rocks were metamorphosed in late Mesozoic or early Tertiary times to form the Owen Stanley Metamorphic Belt and a second, discontinuous, belt which extends from the D'Entrecasteaux Islands to Rossel Island in the extreme southeast. The rocks forming these belts are mainly greenschist facies. To the west, from Middle Jurassic to Upper Cretaceous times, spasmodic deposition of clastic marine sediments and volcanic material occurred, and this was followed by local uplift and minor deformations, and by local metamorphism in a Mobile Belt along the northern flank of the Central Cordillera.

Tertiary

Extensive orogenesis with associated volcanism and clastic sedimentation occurred throughout Lower Tertiary times, and Upper Tertiary times were marked by regional epeirogenic movements, during which large thicknesses of biogenic limestone were deposited in the New Guinea region. In some areas volcanism continued into the Upper Tertiary and the rocks so formed provided

debris for restricted sedimentation. The Papuan Ultramafic Belt is thought to have been emplaced in uppermost Cretaceous or early Tertiary time and it has been suggested that it represents upper mantle and oceanic crust material overthrust from the east. The Ultramafic Belt is separated from the Owen Stanley Metamorphic Belt by a major fault. Eocene sediments unconformably overlie the Owen Stanley Metamorphics in the southwest, and in the north, the Ultramafic Belt is overlain by Lower Miocene marine basic volcanics. The eastern tip of Papua comprises a thick sequence of marine basaltic rocks with minor limestone and other sedimentary rocks.

Extensive deposition of sediments continued along the north coast of Papua from Middle Miocene to Quaternary times, and a thick succession of subaerial pyroclastic rocks and lava flows, formed in Upper Tertiary times on the southern flanks of the Owen Stanley Range, were the source of much of the volcanic greywacke in the Aure Trough, sedimentation was more rapid and more prolonged than elsewhere and a thickness of more than 10,000 m (32,800 ft.) of Miocene and Pliocene volcanic sediments accumulated. To the north, extensive volcanic sedimentation and deposition of limestone occurred along the north New Guinea Coast and to the north and east to form the New Guinea Islands. Major and minor intrusions of granitic and basic rocks occurred in Miocene to Pliocene times and extensive volcanism marked the whole of the period.

Quaternary

Considerable volcanic activity also occurred in Pleistocene times and many areas have remained active to the present day. Principal volcanic areas are eastern Papua and the New Guinea Islands. The extensive volcanic region in Central New Guinea, which was extremely active in Tertiary times, is thought to have now only two non-extinct volcanoes.

There is abundant evidence of rapid vertical movements during the Quaternary Period resulting in some Upper Tertiary marine sediments being found at present day elevations of almost 4,000 m (13,000 ft.) above sea level.

Economic Geology

The only substantial mineral workings up to the present have been of gold and associated precious metals and of copper. The principal gold mining areas were the Morobe Goldfield (Wau, Bulolo, Edie Creek) and Misima Island, but production from both these areas has waned in recent years. There are a large number of smaller gold occurrences throughout most of the Territory.

Copper has in the past been won in some quantity from the Astrolabe Field near Port Moresby and the unworked reserves are currently being assessed. Over the past few years, very large reserves of low-grade porphyry copper have been proved on Bougainville Island, and there is widespread exploration throughout most of the Territory for further deposits of this type. A small amount of manganese ore has been won from a deposit in the Central District, and a number of nickel prospects have been investigated, particular attention being given to the possible existence of lateritic ores overlying the ultramafic rocks. Quite extensive exploration has also been undertaken for bauxite and mineral (beach) sands, and an increasing interest has recently been taken in the non-metallic deposits such as limestone and clays.

In spite of very extensive exploration, oil has not yet been proved in the Territory, although substantial quantities of natural gas are known to occur. Oil exploration, both on-shore and off-shore, is continuing at a high level of activity.

Bibliography:

Rickwood, F. K., 1955. "The Geology of the Western Highlands of New Guinea", *Jour. Geol. Soc. Aust.,* Vol. 2, pp. 63–82.

Thompson, J. E. and Fisher, N. H., 1965. "Mineral Deposits of New Guinea and their Tectonic Setting", *Proc. 8th Comm. Min. and Met. Cong.,* Vol. 6.

* Chief Resident Geologist, Territory of Papua and New Guinea, Port Moresby.

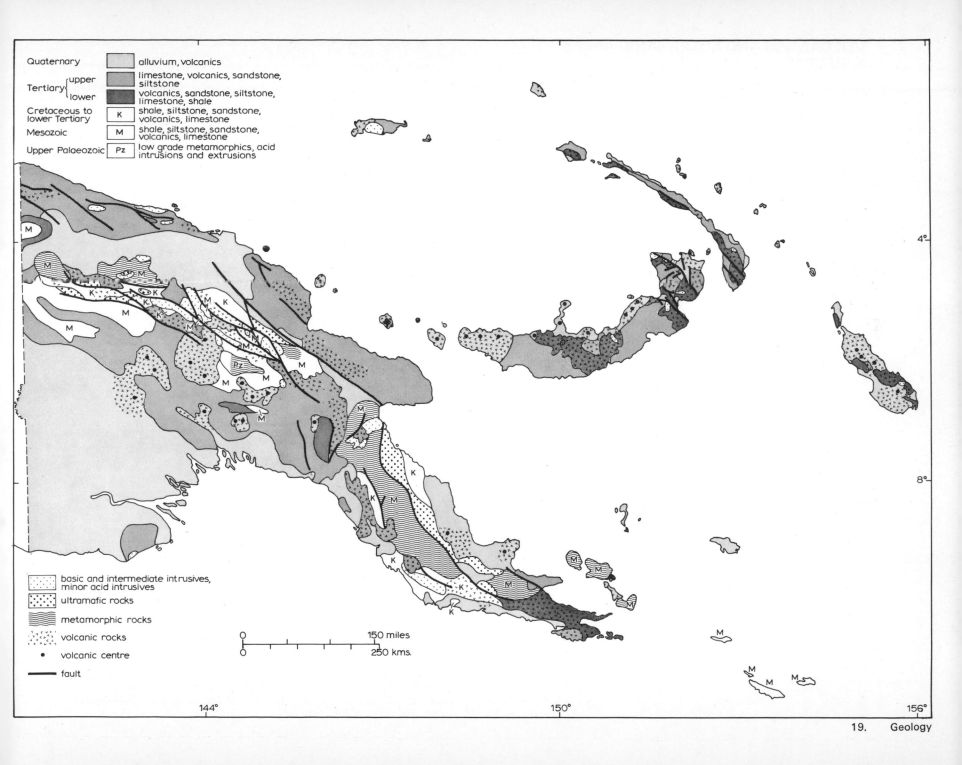

Quaternary — alluvium, volcanics

Tertiary { upper — limestone, volcanics, sandstone, siltstone
lower — volcanics, sandstone, siltstone, limestone, shale

Cretaceous to lower Tertiary — K — shale, siltstone, sandstone, volcanics, limestone

Mesozoic — M — shale, siltstone, sandstone, volcanics, limestone

Upper Palaeozoic — Pz — low grade metamorphics, acid intrusions and extrusions

basic and intermediate intrusives, minor acid intrusives

ultramafic rocks

metamorphic rocks

volcanic rocks

• volcanic centre

— fault

0 ———— 150 miles
0 ———— 250 kms.

4°

8°

144° 150° 156°

19. Geology

VOLCANOES AND SOLFATARIC AREAS
A. RENWICK

Map 20 shows all the volcanoes and solfataric areas which are currently regarded as non-extinct. In sub-dividing the volcanoes into those with and those without recorded eruptions, it has been decided to list in the former category those, such as Doma Peaks (38), which have probably erupted in what are normally termed historic times but of which there is no established written record.

1. Mt. Lamington
2. Mt. Trafalgar
3. Mt. Victory
4. Lower Musa River
5. Mt. Goropu
6. Iamelele (Fergusson Island)
7. Dei Dei (Fergusson Island)
8. Dobu (Normanby Island)
9. Mt. Loloru (Bougainville)
10. Mt. Bagana (Bougainville)
11. Mt. Balbi (Bougainville)
12. Ambitle (Feni Islands)
13. Lihir
14. Rabaul
15. Ulawun
16. Lolobau
17. Bamus
18. Gallosuelo
19. Walo
20. Pago
21. Garbuna
22. Garua (Talasea Harbour)
23. Bola
24. Benda
25. Garove
26. Narage
27. Langila
28. Sakar
29. Ritter
30. Talo
31. Long Island
32. Tuluman (Manus)
33. Kar Kar Island
34. Manam Island
35. Bam Island
36. North north east of Kar Kar Island (submarine)
37. Mt. Yelia
38. Doma Peaks

Bibliography:
Fisher, N. H., 1957. *"Catalogue of the Active Volcanoes of the World including Solfataric Fields: Pt. V. Melanesia"*. Int. Volc. Assoc., Naples, Italy.
Taylor, G. A., 1958. "The 1951 Eruption of Mt. Lamington, Papua", *Bur. Min. Resour. Aust. Bull.*, 38.

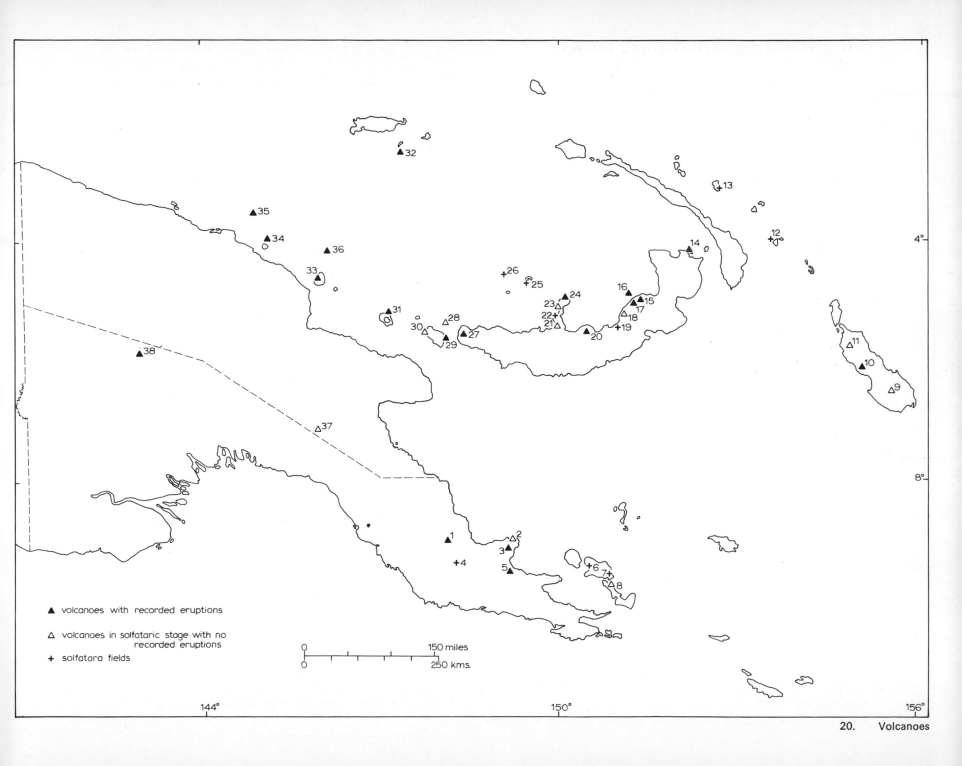

▲ volcanoes with recorded eruptions

△ volcanoes in solfataric stage with no
   recorded eruptions

+ solfatara fields

150 miles

0

250 kms.

20.　Volcanoes

EARTHQUAKES *DAVID DENHAM* *

The most active seismic area is associated with the New Britain Island Arc. A large percentage of the earthquakes occurring in the region originate from this area. The island of New Britain is similar to many island arcs which surround the active margins of the Pacific Ocean. It is a gently curved feature with a line of volcanoes located on the northern concave side and a deep ocean trench, which reaches a maximum depth of about 9,140 m. (30,000 ft.) at the convex southern side of the island. The seismic activity associated with this arc is highest near east New Britain. The majority of the shocks are located in the 40–60 km. (25–37 miles) depth range. In general the shallow earthquakes lie at the southern side of the island and the active seismic zone dips to the north under the island. The deepest shocks associated with the zone occur under the Bismarck Sea at depths down to 600 km. (370 miles).

The second most active area is situated between Bougainville and New Ireland. This region contains most of the deep earthquakes occurring in the Territory. The seismic zone dips to the northwest under the axis of the Solomon Islands. There is a region of relatively low seismicity in the centre of the Solomon Chain to the east of the map border. This region corresponds to the absence of any deep trench in this part of the Solomon Sea. Still further east around San Cristoval island an ocean trench is well developed and seismic activity increases.

One unexpected feature revealed on the map is the line of shallow earthquakes stretching across the Bismarck Sea from the southwest end of New Ireland to the New Guinea coast near Wewak. This line of epicentres, which is called the Bismarck Sea Seismic Lineation, is very well defined and the maximum width of the feature appears to be only about 40 km. (25 miles). This zone is quite active and an average of at least one earthquake of magnitude six or greater originates from it each year. It does not correspond to any known topographic feature on the floor of the ocean.

The distribution of earthquakes under the New Guinea mainland is very complicated. The New Britain Island Arc does not extend westward beyond Manam Island and a new trend situated almost *en echelon* starts at the Huon Peninsula and extends westwards into West Irian. This appears to be independent of the New Britain Island Arc and the earthquakes associated with this zone dip to the south under the main island of New Guinea. In West Irian the seismic zones are not well defined and most of the earthquakes are shallow events.

Two important zones of minor seismicity are revealed on the map. One is associated with the West Melanesian Arc, which is situated at the northern edge of the region and stretches from the north of New Ireland to the West Irian border with its convex side facing north. Only a few earthquakes occur in this zone, which is probably caused by the interaction of the Pacific Plate with the northern edge of the New Guinea region. The second zone stretches from the volcanic region in southeast Papua to the Solomon Islands and appears to be associated with the ridge across the Solomon Sea. The significance of this zone is not yet fully understood.

Earthquakes pose a serious hazard to buildings, particularly if the movement is large and the epicentre shallow. In areas of high earthquake risk, special precautions should be taken to ensure that buildings constructed in these zones are designed to resist earthquake vibrations. The areas of high risk are New Britain, Bougainville, the southern part of New Ireland, the mainland of New Guinea (north of the political boundary between Papua and New Guinea) and the southeastern tip of Papua.

In recent years three series of damaging earthquakes have occurred in New Guinea. These were the Kokopo earthquakes of 1967, the West New Britain earthquake of 1968 and the Wewak earthquakes of 1968. The damage caused by these earthquakes totalled more than $500,000.

The surface of the earth can be regarded as being divided into large, relatively stable "plates" which move around the globe. The New Guinea–Solomon Islands region is located in the zone of inter-action between the westward-spreading Pacific plate and the northward-moving plate containing the Australian continent and the southeast Indian Ocean. The plates usually move at velocities of 1 to 5 cm/year and where they interact seismic activity is manifest. In the New Guinea region the main activity can be associated with the northward-moving Australian plate, which has its leading edge along the north coast of New Guinea and the northern boundary of the Solomon Sea. The map locates the epicentres of earthquakes recorded between 1958 and 1968 which had a force of 5·5 or greater.

* Observer-in-Charge, Bureau of Mineral Resources, Geophysical Observatory, Port Moresby.

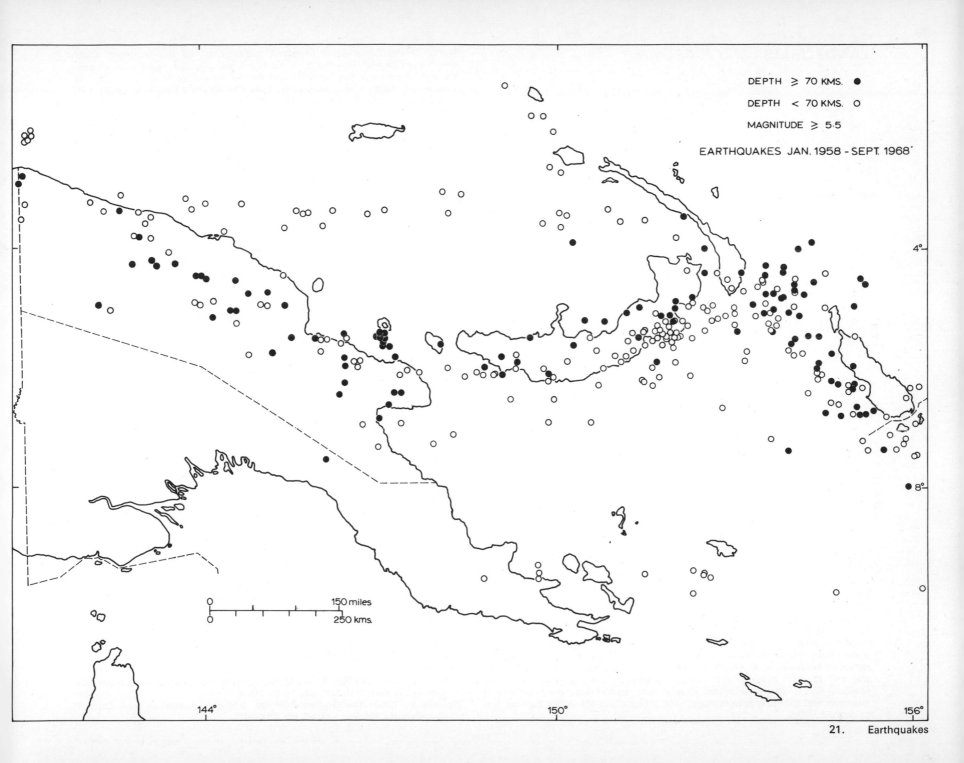

DEPTH ≥ 70 KMS. ●

DEPTH < 70 KMS. O

MAGNITUDE ≥ 5·5

EARTHQUAKES JAN. 1958 - SEPT. 1968

4°

8°

150 miles

250 kms.

144°

150°

156°

21.   Earthquakes

LANDFORMS *M. J. F. BROWN*

Papua and New Guinea is characterized by a wide variety of landforms, many of which date from Pleistocene or Recent times. The overall distribution of landforms is known but, in spite of important contributions by a few geomorphologists and the Division of Land Research, C.S.I.R.O., it is not yet possible to advance far beyond physiographic descriptions.

Mountains The most prominent physiographic feature is the Central Cordillera which extends continuously from Semenandjung Doreri (the Vogelkop) in Irian Barat to the Owen Stanley Range in Papua, and is continued in the drowned chain of the Louisiade Archipelago. It is broadest in the west where wide intramontane plains at elevations of 5,000–6,000 ft. are separated by mountain ridges of up to 14,000 ft. The plains are generally strike-aligned and are covered with alluvium and volcanic detritus ; there are extensive gravel spreads, lacustrine deposits and alluvial fans. In the east the cordillera is narrower and generally lower, though Mt. Victoria and Mt. Albert Edward rise to over 13,000 ft.

North of the Sepik-Ramu-Markham fault trough is the Northern Chain which runs parallel with the main cordillera but is not so wide, lofty or continuous. It includes the Torricelli and Prince Alexander Mountains, and the Adalbert, Finisterre and Sarawaged ranges. The latter are continued structurally by the mountainous backbone of New Britain.

Post-Miocene Volcanic Landforms dominate much of the landscape of Papua and New Guinea. On the mainland, with a few exceptions, volcanic activity is now extinct. In the Highlands the volcanic mountains of Hagen and Giluwe rise to over 13,000 ft. and have glaciated summits. One of the most impressive volcanoes of western Papua is Mt. Bosavi, a very smooth dissected symmetrical cone with nearly perfect radial drainage, rising to over 9,000 ft. It carries a crater, the floor of which lies about 4,000 ft. below the rim, and is surrounded by a plain of volcanic detritus—the Great Papuan Plateau. In northern Papua volcanic mountains include the Hydrographers Range, Lamington, Victory and Trafalgar. That activity has not ceased is shown by a major eruption of Mt. Victory about 1880 and the disastrous Peléan type eruption of Lamington in 1951.

The majority of the active volcanoes are confined to the Bismarck Volcanic Belt which extends in an arc along the north side of New Guinea and New Britain. On the north coast of New Britain the volcanoes are of the explosive type, and catastrophic eruptions have occurred in recent times forming calderas, of which the Willaumez Peninsula and Blanche Bay are fine examples.

Glacial Landscapes Although there are no permanent snow or ice fields, as in Irian Barat, Pleistocene glaciation affected the highest mountain areas. These include Mt. Capella and Sirius near the western border, Mt. Hagen, Giluwe and Wilhelm in the Highlands, Mt. Sarawaged on the Huon Peninsula and Mts. Victoria and Albert Edward in the Owen Stanleys. A Pleistocene snow line at 11,500–12,000 ft. has been deduced for the Mt. Wilhelm area (Reiner 1960 : 502).

Karst landscapes occur in wide areas of western Papua and New Britain. South of the Muller Range lie mainly limestone formations ; nearly all the prominent ridges and some extensive plateaux are limestone. There is a wide variety of karst, including 'kegelkarst', tower and doline, pyramid and doline, and arete and doline types. "... there seems to be an altitudinal zonation of karst in New Guinea, though at each level the picture is not a simple one, complicated as it is by the cross-cutting influences of lithology, structure and evolutionary history" (Jennings & Bik, 1962 : 1038).

Alluvial Plains, Swamps and Coastal Plains The vast plains of the Fly, Turama, Bamu and Kikori rivers form part of the most extensive swamplands in the world. Of comparable size are the swamps of the Sepik. Smaller swamp areas occur adjacent to the coast, especially in southern Papua, most of which is believed to be an area of subsidence. Floodplain landforms of great variety are found. The Markham and Ramu valleys have braided river systems and large alluvial fans at the mouths of tributary valleys. The higher alluvial plains include the Sepik grasslands and the Oriomo Plateau.

Raised Coral Reefs are a feature of the north coast of New Guinea, the south coast of New Britain, Bougainville, eastern New Ireland and many smaller islands including the Trobriands and the Louisiade Archipelago. The north coast of New Guinea is one of active elevation and raised reefs are found up to 2,000 ft. on the Huon Peninsula. In New Britain there are tilted raised reefs rising in terraces to 2,000 ft. inland.

Bibliography

Jennings, J. N., and Bik, M. J., 1962. 'Karst Morphology in Australian New Guinea', *Nature*, Vol. 194, pp. 1036–1038.

Reiner, E., 1960. 'The Glaciation of Mt. Wilhelm, Australian New Guinea', *Geographical Review*, Vol. 50, pp. 491–503.

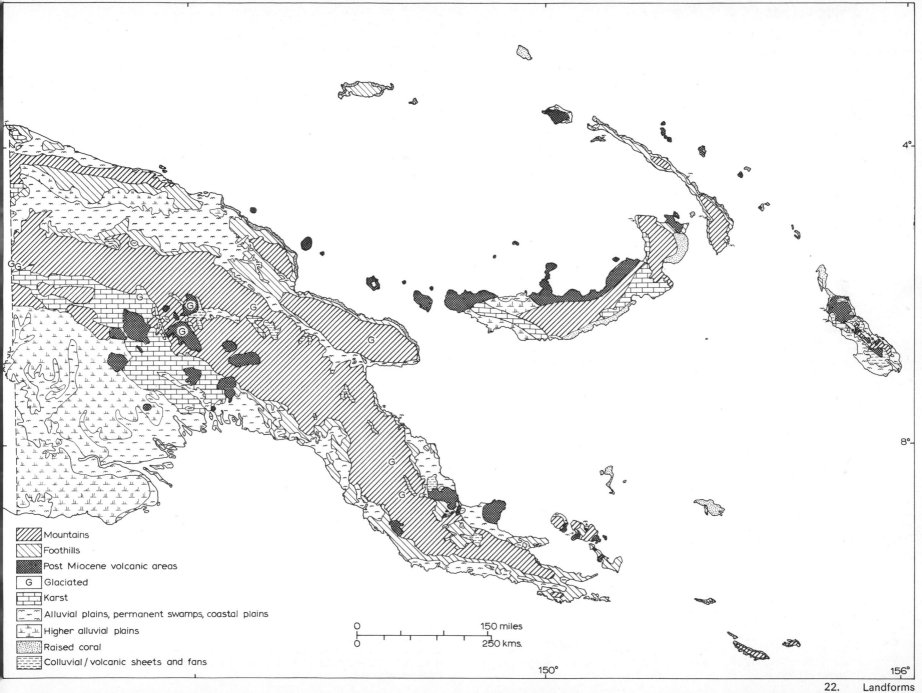

Mountains

Foothills

Post Miocene volcanic areas

G Glaciated

Karst

Alluvial plains, permanent swamps, coastal plains

Higher alluvial plains

Raised coral

Colluvial / volcanic sheets and fans

150 miles

250 kms.

22. Landforms

SOILS *H. A. HAANTJENS* *

This soil map is derived from a map at 1:2,500,000 of the whole island of New Guinea (Haantjens *et al'*, 1967) and updated by minor alterations based on the results of reconnaissance surveys carried out from 1964 to 1968 by the CSIRO, Division of Land Research. The map must still be considered a first approximation, based on very incomplete data, and in need of much correction and refinement.

Soil Associations of the High Mountains

Li/aH.—Mountain summits at 3,000–4,500 m. (10,000–14,500 ft.) with relict glacial features and alpine vegetation. Lithosols and Alpine Humus soils co-dominant, also rock outcrop.

bPo/aH.—Rugged mountains of limestone and other rocks between 1,000 and 3,000 m. (3,300–10,000 ft.). Mossy lower montane and montane forest. Alpine Humus soils dominate at higher altitude, Brown Podzolic soils at lower altitude, both with associated Lithosols.

hbL/gP/R.—Mountain ranges, valleys and hilly uplands between 1,500 and 3,000 m. (5,000–10,000 ft.). Lower montane forest and grassland. Humic Brown Latosols on well drained sites, Gleyed Pelosols on fine-textured impervious sediments, Rendzinas on limestone. Also Meadow Podzolic and Lateritic soils on old valley fills, Bog soils in swamps and minor Alluvial soils.

IA/B.—Extinct volcanoes, ash plains and ash-covered hilly uplands between 1,500 and 3,000 m. (5,000–10,000 ft.). Lower montane forest and grassland. Latosolic Andosols dominant, merging into Bog and Half Bog soils in depressions and on level plains.

Reg/aBf/hbL.—Very rugged mountains between 500 and 3,000 m. (1,600–10,000 ft.). Lowland hill forest and lower montane forest. Regosolic Brown soils dominant, with Acid Brown Forest soils, Humic Brown Latosols, and, at lower altitude also Red and Yellow Latosols on more stable sites.

Soil Associations of the Low Mountains and Hills

Bf/Reg.—Closely dissected mountains between 500 and 1,200 m. (1,600–4,000 ft.). Mainly lowland hill forest. Brown Forest soils and Regosolic Brown soils co-dominant, some Red and Yellow Latosols on stable crests and lower slopes, Rendzinas on limestone, and Gleyed Pelosols on impervious sedimentary rocks.

Bf/gP.—Irregular hilly land on sedimentary rock, up to 900 m. (3,000 ft.) altitude. Lowland hill forest and secondary vegetation. Brown Forest soils on well-drained sites, Gleyed Pelosols on impervious rocks and gentler slopes. Locally Red and Yellow Latosols and Meadow Podzolic soils on wider crests.

ryL/Reg.—Steep-sided hill ridges with broad and/or accordant crests, and low block mountains of basic/ultra basic rock up to 800 m. (2,600 ft.) altitude. Mostly lowland hill forest. Red and Yellow Latosols mainly on crests and upper slopes, Regosolic Brown soils on lower slopes with Acid Brown Forest soils and some Lithosols. Some Lateritic soils and Gleyed Pelosols on impervious rocks, and Rendzinas on limestone.

R/Tr.—Limestone hills below 1,200 m. (4,000 ft.) and raised coral reefs. Lowland hill forest, with deciduous trees and grassland in drier areas. Rendzinas are dominant and occur on steep slopes and young reefs. The associated Terra Rossas are on older surfaces and grade into Red and Yellow Latosols. Much rock outcrop.

A/Li.—Active and dormant volcanoes up to 1,800 m. (6,000 ft.) high, with adjoining plains and ash-covered hills and mountains. Rainforest and seral vegetation. Andosols dominant ranging from young grey sands to older brown sandy clays; Lithosols on summit areas and young lava flows; some Acid Brown Forest Soils and Red Latosols on older lavas.

Li/S/G.—Hills and valleys below 600 m. (2,000 ft.). Seasonally dry, with mainly savanna, grassland and mixed deciduous forest. Many Lithosols on hill slopes, Solonetzic and related planosolic soils on foot slopes and terrace benches, locally with Lateritic soils. Grumusols in alluvial plains together with Alluvial soils.

Soil Associations of the Plains

ryL/aBf/La.—Slightly to strongly dissected plains on Pleistocene sediments below 400 m. (1,300 ft.). Lowland rainforest, some grassland. Red and Yellow Latosols dominant, with Acid Brown Forest soils on dissection slopes. Some Lateritic soils on poorer drained surfaces, and Alluvial and Half Bog Soils on associated flood-plains.

pLa/La/mPo.—Gently undulating plains on Pleistocene sediments below 40 m. (130 ft.). Seasonally dry, with mainly savanna and grassland. Podzolic Lateritic soils, with some Lateritic soils on highest parts and Meadow Podzolic soils in wetter, lower situations. Half Bog and Bog soils in associated flood-plain swamps.

mPo/gP.—Slightly to strongly dissected plains on Pleistocene sediments below 300 m. (1,000 ft.). Grassland, forest and swamp vegetation. Meadow Podzolic and a few Lateritic soils on older surfaces, Gleyed Pelosols on younger surfaces and slopes. Some Alluvial and Half Bog soils on associated flood-plains.

Al/hB.—Young alluvial plains below 300 m. Mainly tall alluvial plain forest. Alluvial soils dominant, with Half Bog soils in wettest areas. Some Gleyed Pelosols on older sediments.

hB/B/Al.—Freshwater swamps and poorly drained alluvial plains below 150 m. Mainly swamp vegetation of many kinds. Half Bog and Bog soils dominant, with Alluvial soils on better drained plains.

saPMS.—Tidal mangrove plains at sea level. Saline peat, mud and sand.

Note: A cyclostyled description of the major soil groups is available on request from the editors.

* Division of Land Research, CSIRO, Canberra, Australia.

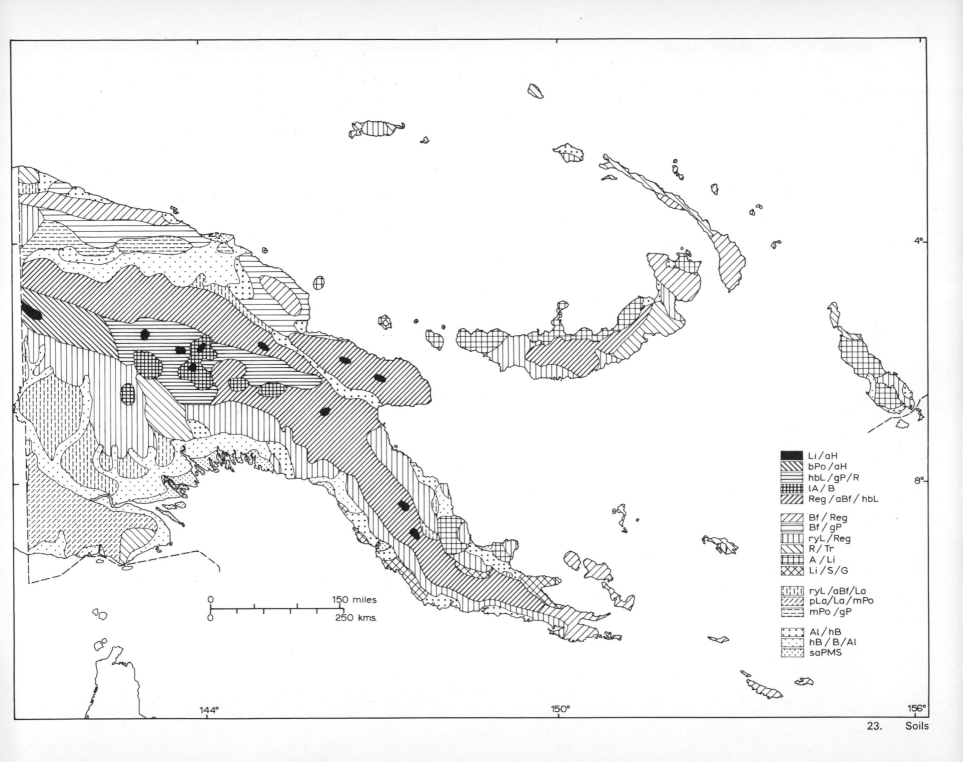

▨	Li / aH
◩	bPo / aH
▤	hbL / gP / R
▦	lA / B
▨	Reg / aBf / hbL
▨	Bf / Reg
▤	Bf / gP
▥	ryL / Reg
◩	R / Tr
▦	A / Li
▨	Li / S / G
▦	ryL / aBf / La
▨	pLa / La / mPo
▤	mPo / gP
▨	Al / hB
▨	hB / B / Al
▨	saPMS

150 miles

250 kms.

144°   150°   156°

4°

8°

23.   Soils

RAINFALL   *DOREEN HART* *

All basic data for Maps 24 and 25 were provided by the Australian Bureau of Meteorology, Melbourne, who maintain records covering varying periods of time for a number of rainfall stations throughout the area. Though important improvements have been made in recent years, the over-all network of rainfall stations in Papua and New Guinea is still far from adequate. Moreover the length of time during which recording has taken place is not constant throughout the area, and the calculated means therefore are not strictly comparable. Most of the longer records, 25 years and over, are found on the coast in towns and plantation areas, while inland records are generally much shorter and there are still areas, for example in the sparsely peopled Western District, where no rainfall records have ever been taken. In such areas extrapolation between existing widely-spaced stations was necessary, using information on relief, vegetation and general field knowledge. All maps presented here are part of wider studies of rainfall in the southwest Pacific and therefore in the drawing of isohyets for Papua and New Guinea, data from Irian Barat, provided by the Meteorologisch en Geofysisch Bureau te Hollandia, were also taken into consideration. Annual means were calculated for years up to and including 1963 for stations with a minimum of five years' complete data. This gave a basic network for plotting of 207 stations. A considerable amount of inferior data was also used as a supplement.

Papua and New Guinea lie within the heavy precipitation belt of the Humid Tropics and well over half the Territory receives 100 ins. (2,450 mm.) rainfall or more per annum. The distribution, however, is far from uniform and the range of means is large, as the following extreme examples show :

Station	No. of Years	Annual Mean	
		ins.	*(mm.)*
Gasmata	21	239·23	(6076)
Kikori	38	226·80	(5761)
Rigo	34	44·49	(1130)
Port Moresby	42	39·17	(995)

Distinct dry and extra wet zones exist. Though extreme dryness is rare, with only a small area along the coast of central Papua experiencing less than 40 ins. (1016 mm.) annual rainfall, there are extensive areas which are relatively dry in the lower Fly and Sepik valleys and the eastern part of the central highlands extending into the Markham valley. In complete contrast are the two major belts of excessive rainfall which receive over 200 ins. (5080 mm.) a year. These occur along the southern edge of the central cordillera, from the Gulf of Papua into Irian Barat and along the southern coast of New Britain.

Using only the basic network of 207 stations, mean monthly totals for 3 four-monthly periods January–April, May–August and September–December were plotted. The periods chosen correspond roughly to the main climatic seasons, discussed more fully below. A single maximum of rainfall is typical of Papua and New Guinea and over most of the Territory this peak occurs in the early part of the year. Important exceptions to this are the belts of extremely heavy rainfall mentioned above and other similar, but smaller, areas on the west coast of Bougainville and around the Huon Gulf ; here the maximum occurs mid-year. For the rest of the Territory this mid-year period is the time of least rainfall. A double maximum of rainfall, a common feature at low latitudes, is rare in Papua and New Guinea. Its widest distribution is in the Southern Highlands with smaller isolated occurrences around Rabaul, Wewak, Manus, Lae and Milne Bay.

The irregularities of rainfall distribution observed are due largely to the varying effects of relief acting on the prevailing airmasses. The main island of New Guinea, with its highly accidented surface, acts as a particularly strong climatic control, and within the central cordillera, whose mountains in places rise to

* Formerly Research Assistant, Research School of Pacific Studies, Australian National University.

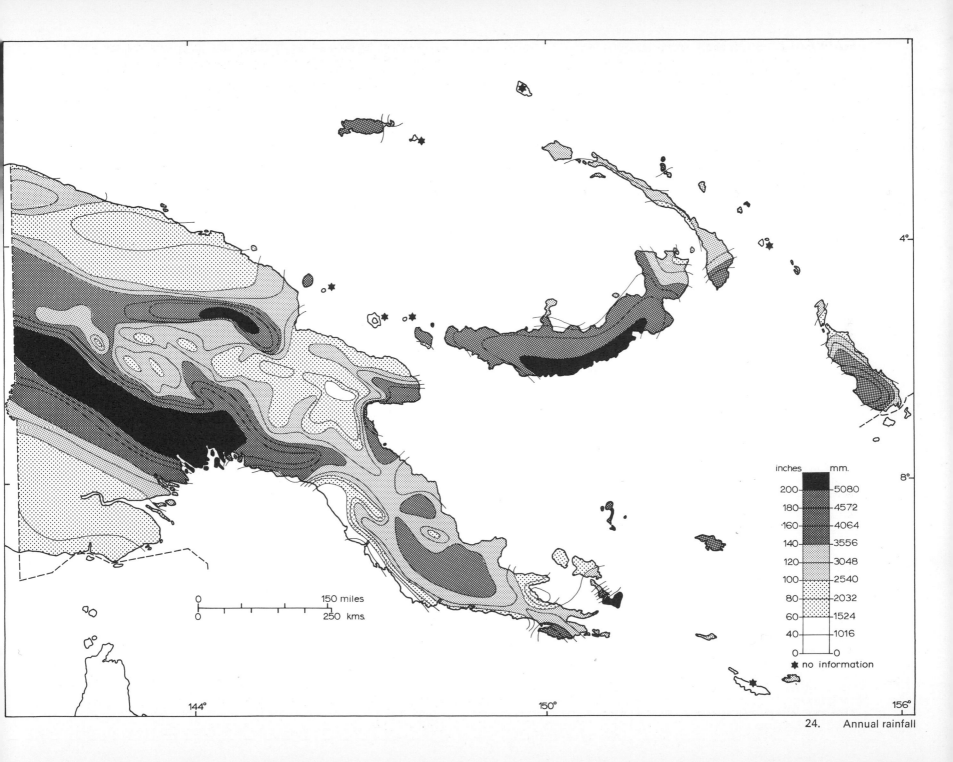

inches	mm.
200	5080
180	4572
160	4064
140	3556
120	3048
100	2540
80	2032
60	1524
40	1016
0	0

★ no information

0   150 miles
0   250 kms.

24.   Annual rainfall

near the snow line, the effect of topography seems to dominate climate producing completely independent local circulations.

Two main surface systems pass over the remainder of Papua and New Guinea at different times of the year giving distinct rainfall seasons. The 'Southeasterly' system, traditionally known as the 'Trades', is the most dominant in that it largely determines the pattern of rainfall for the whole year. Advancing from the south in May and retreating again in August, it is accompanied by strong steady winds which produce marked wind and lee effects. The moisture content of these winds by the time they reach Papua and New Guinea is much lower than at their source, so that when they blow parallel to the coast and the general lines of relief, as in central Papua, little rainfall results. Nevertheless when confronted with a barrier, such as the mountains of New Britain or the southern face of the Central Cordillera, they can produce extremely heavy rainfall. The topographic barrier of the Central Cordillera is so great that the southeasterlies, rather than penetrating the highlands, bank up against them, causing increased rainfall over the foothills and plains to the south.

As the southeasterlies retreat their place is gradually taken by the 'Perturbation Belt' which reaches its maximum development in the early part of the year. The late-year period is essentially transitional between the two main systems. The 'Perturbation Belt' is characterized by westerly moving vortical circulations separated by zones of convergence and causes highly localized heavy rainfall with little wind and lee effects. As with the southeasterlies this system does not appear to penetrate deep into the Central Highlands.

The map of rainfall regimes (Map 25d), summarizing the rainfall types of Papua and New Guinea, developed from a study of rainfall seasonality in the southwest Pacific using harmonic analysis (Fitzpatrick, Hart and Brookfield, 1966). Such analysis, by eliminating many of the random elements in the monthly means, gives a reasonably objective basis for the areal differentiation of seasonality.

Harmonic analysis was applied to mean monthly rainfall data for a selection of stations, and from this mean weekly values were produced. It was then possible to evaluate the frequencies of heavy (over 2 ins. (50 mm.)) intermediate (1–2 ins. (25–50 mm.)) and light (below 1 in. (25 mm.)) rainfall. Stations were then grouped into 7 classes*, ranging from *Continuously wet* to *Continuously light* according to the duration of each rainfall frequency. Owing to the general lack of adequate data in so complex an area it was not possible to map regimes over much of the Central Highlands.

As would be expected the *Continuously wet* and the *Moderate range–heave to intermediate* regimes together cover a large part of the Territory, coinciding broadly with the areas of very high rainfall. Here seasonality is not marked. The areas of high seasonality, often an important factor in agriculture with crops favouring a dry period for harvesting, fall within the relatively dry zones. Regimes of this group comprise *Large range, heavy to light, heavy dominant, Large range, heavy to light, light dominant* and the *Moderate range, intermediate to light* regime of Central Papua and the Markham valley.

In the Humid Tropics, where rain, when it occurs, is characteristically in heavy falls, one would not expect to find a *Continuously intermediate* regime, yet there are two small areas where such conditions prevail—around Wewak and Rabaul—and there may be others. No explanation for these occurrences can be offered at present. In terms of human occupation such a regime is of considerable potential in a country where a surfeit of rainfall is a problem more frequently encountered than a dearth.

It must be stressed that certain parts of the maps presented here are no more than broad generalizations. It is to be hoped that within the near future improvements in the network of rainfall stations, as well as the lengthening period of records available at existing stations, will make the production of more detailed maps possible. At the same time research into upper air as well as surface climatic data should throw further light on the problems of rainfall controls.

Bibliography:

Brookfield, H. C., and Hart, D., 1966. *Rainfall in the Tropical Southwest Pacific,* Canberra.

Brookfield, H. C., with Hart, D., (in press). *Melanesia: a Geographical Interpretation,* London.

Fitzpatrick, E. A., Hart, D. and Brookfield, H. C., 1966. 'Seasonality of rainfall in the tropical southwest Pacific'. *Erdkunde,* Vol. 20, pp. 181–194.

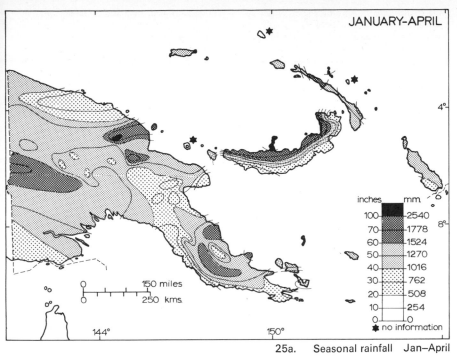

JANUARY-APRIL

inches		mm.
100		2540
70		1778
60		1524
50		1270
40		1016
30		762
20		508
10		254
0		0

150 miles
250 kms.

★ no information

25a.   Seasonal rainfall   Jan–April

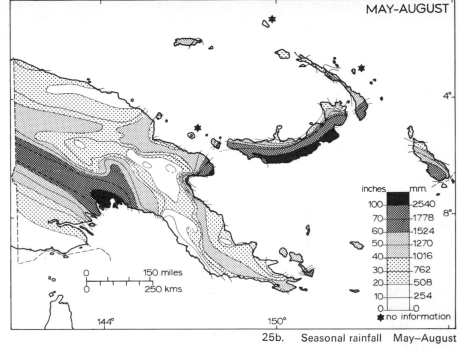

MAY-AUGUST

inches		mm.
100		2540
70		1778
60		1524
50		1270
40		1016
30		762
20		508
10		254
0		0

150 miles
250 kms.

★ no information

25b.   Seasonal rainfall   May–August

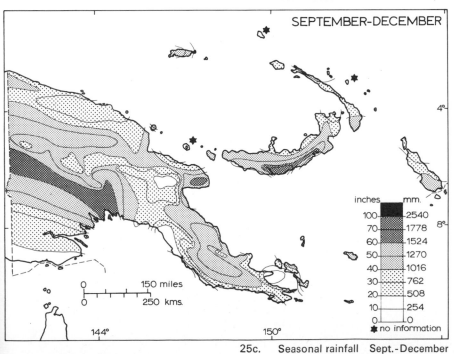

SEPTEMBER-DECEMBER

inches		mm.
100		2540
70		1778
60		1524
50		1270
40		1016
30		762
20		508
10		254
0		0

150 miles
250 kms.

★ no information

25c.   Seasonal rainfall   Sept.-December

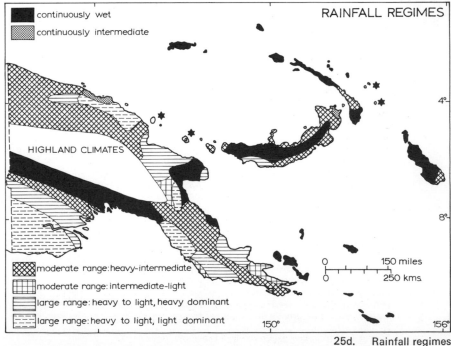

RAINFALL REGIMES

continuously wet

continuously intermediate

HIGHLAND CLIMATES

moderate range: heavy-intermediate

moderate range: intermediate-light

large range: heavy to light, heavy dominant

large range: heavy to light, light dominant

150 miles
250 kms.

25d.   Rainfall regimes

VEGETATION   *ROSS G. ROBBINS* *

A natural vegetation, predominantly rainforest, still covers about three-quarters of Papua and New Guinea. Total plant species number some 20,000 with strongest affinities to the Indo-Malaysian flora but with interesting Australian and Pacific elements also present. Plant communities range from coastal mangroves and strand forests to lowland savannas and grasslands and woody and herbaceous swamps; from lowland forests to mid-montane oaks, laurels, beeches and conifers. True montane "mossy" forests give way to sub-alpine scrubs and finally alpine tussock grassland and tundra.

Mangroves occupy mudflats of all large river estuaries and most form a mixed woodland of stilt-rooted trees subject to a 2–3 ft. rise and fall of tides. The optimum is a well-developed *Rhizophora-Bruguiera* forest with trees 100 ft. in height. In brackish reaches Nipa palm becomes dominant.

Herbaceous swamps cover large backplains along many rivers. "Pit pit" (*Phragmites*), and wild sugarcane (*Saccharum*) form dense stands 20 ft. high while, with greater inundation, masses of floating and trailing grasses lead to aquatic communities of water ferns, sedges, weeds and water lilies growing around open lakes.

Swampwoodland is best characterized by the vast tracts of mosquito-infested sago palm (*Metroxylon*) groves where the seasonal watertable drops just below the surface in the dry period. The palms grow in clumps with low over-arching fronds and associated swamp-tolerant trees. The pith of the mature palm trunk yields a crude starch which is the staple diet over much of the year for the local inhabitants.

Savanna of some three of four species of scattered *Eucalyptus* trees, over a ground cover of kangaroo grass is a feature of much of the low-lying dry southern Papuan shelf. This becomes a swamp-savanna in the Fly delta with paperback trees (*Melaleucca*) and mixed grasses.

Regrowth and grassland is the vegetation pattern of settled inland valleys and particularly the coast. Such vegetation is the result of shifting agriculture. Garden plots are first cleared from the virgin forest and after cropping allowed to revert back to woody regrowth. Further interference results in a patchwork of forest remnants, secondary regrowth, open grassland stages and current garden plots.

Grassland which is found in both the lowlands and highlands represents man's greatest impact upon the vegetation. They are probably man-made disclimaxes. Dominated by *Themeda* and *Imperata,* the short grassland tracts are maintained by annual firing. Tall grasslands, notably of swordgrass (*Miscanthus*) in the highlands, may be regarded as a regrowth phase before final conversion to short grassland. Little used in the native economy except for hunting, the grasslands have a potential for cattle and reafforestation.

Lowland rainforest, by far the most common vegetation type, is found up to 3,000 ft. in all areas with a well-distributed rainfall over 60 ins. per annum. While several associations, including areas of Malayan dipterocarp species, can be recognized over a variety of soils and topography, for the most part they are of very mixed composition. Species include many timber trees—*Pometia, Intsia, Dysoxylum, Celtis, Canarium, Terminalia* and a host of others. Five forest layers (three tree layers followed by a shrub and ground layer) may be recognized. Flange-buttressed trunks, palms and rattans, woody lianes and epiphytes are all characteristic.

Lower montane forest is found in mountain slopes between 3,000 ft. and 9,000·10,000 ft. It is recognized by a reduction in structure to two tree layers and a change in floristic composition and includes oak-laurel (*Castanopsis-Cryptocarya*) forests, mixed forests with species belonging to the Elaeocarpaceae and Cunnoniaceae and pure stands of southern beech (*Nothofagus*).

Montane forest does not begin until at least 9,000 ft. or the altitude where a single tree layer becomes the optimum. This community is often confused with the misted mossy aspects of lower montane forest at lower levels. The low dense canopy is at 35 ft. and includes Myrtaceae, conifers and other temperate species representatives. Montane forest grades into a sub-alpine aspect at 11,000 ft. where the conifers are often emergent. It is followed by sub-alpine scrub and grasses to about 13,500 ft.

Alpine vegetation of tussock grasses, alpine herbs and mosses occurs only above 13,500 ft. Southern temperate families have interesting representatives here. Tussock grassland (*Danthonia, Poa*) dominates, with small alpine bogs and a tundra-like vegetation of ferns, lichens and mosses which is found almost to the summit of Mt. Wilhelm at 14,793 ft. Permanent snowfields are found only in West Irian.

Bibliography:

Good, R., 1964. *The Geography of Flowering Plants,* Chapter 12, London.
Womersley, J. S., and McAdam, J. B., 1957. *The Forest and Forest Conditions in the Territory of Papua and New Guinea,* Port Moresby.

* Senior Lecturer in Biology, University of Papua and New Guinea.

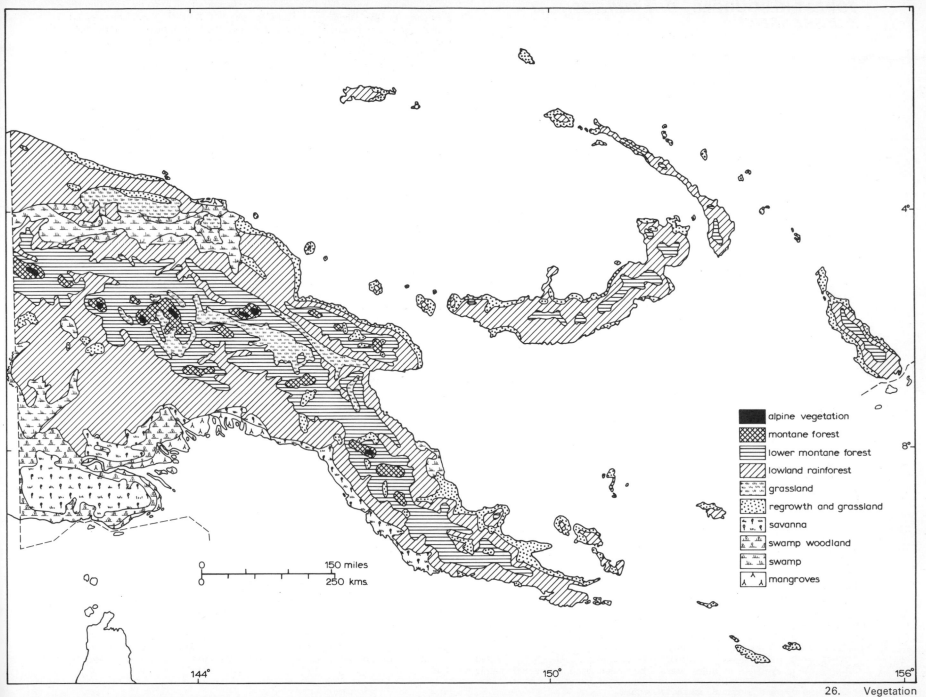

■	alpine vegetation
▨	montane forest
☰	lower montane forest
⫽	lowland rainforest
≡	grassland
⫶	regrowth and grassland
⸭	savanna
⫶	swamp woodland
⫶	swamp
ʌ	mangroves

150 miles

250 kms.

144°   150°   156°

4°

8°

26.   Vegetation

FOREST RESOURCES *D. H. McINTOSH and K. J. GRANGER* *

by preliminary photo-interpretation supplemented in places by reports published by the Division of Land Research C.S.I.R.O. From this limited knowledge of composition, extent and access, the area appears to be productive but more intensive studies must be undertaken before development can be planned.

Forested area on mountainous terrain (59,400,000 acres). This category includes the remaining forested areas and has been delineated from aerial photographs and from field reports. At present levels of technology and utilization the productivity of these areas is severely limited by virtue of the broken and mountainous terrain. Small areas of forest of known and possible local importance within this area have been indicated by symbols.

Unforested (34,600,000 acres). The remainder of the country includes natural and anthropogenic grassland, savanna, swamp and present or recent cultivation, and has no immediate forest potential apart from small areas of local importance indicated by symbols.

The forests of Papua and New Guinea represent a great natural resource which is gradually being opened up for development. From reconnaissance flights and air photo interpretation the most promising forest areas are selected and assessed, often with the aid of a helicopter. These surveys result in detailed maps and reports designed to give a potential investor sufficient information for development planning.

The forests are owned by the indigenous people, and the fragmented ownership patterns existing in the traditional situation are such that some form of unified tenure is necessary for successful development. To this end, the Administration purchases the Timber Rights from the owners for periods of up to 40 years. As at the 30th June, 1969 the Administration held Timber Rights over some 3,800,000 acres. With the tenure assured, and the resource assessed, these timber areas are made available for development aimed at satisfying local and export demands for forest products.

The rich mixture of species found in the rain forests of Papua and New Guinea brings its own problems, and integrated industries are necessary for successful utilization. To this end, research is being conducted, both within the country and elsewhere, into the properties and uses of New Guinea's timbers. This work has recently been extended to the field of chip production for pulp wood.

The main species of present economic interest occur within two broad zones, namely the lowland area, below 3,000 feet, and the mid-montane area, from 3,000 ft. to 9,000 ft. In the lowland area the main economic species are *Pometia spp.* (Taun), *Eucalyptus deglupta* (Kamarere), *Intsia spp.* (Kwila), *Dracontomelum* (N.G. Walnut), *Anisoptera polyandra, Hopea spp.* and *Agathis spp.* (Kauri Pine). Within the mid-montane zone *Araucaria hunsteinii* (Klinkii Pine) and *Araucaria cunninghamii* (Hoop Pine) are the main economic species, occurring in limited areas, with the hardwoods, such as *Nothofagus spp.* (Beech) also being utilized.

Permanent Forest Areas have been established in both zones to perpetuate and increase the natural resource. The two lowland stations, Keravat (near Rabaul) and Mt. Lawes (near Port Moresby) are being planted with *Tectona grandis* (Teak) and indigenous species of *Eucalyptus* and *Terminalia*. The mid-montane stations are Bulolo, where the *Araucaria* species are being planted on a large scale, and Asaro (near Goroka) which is being planted with exotic *Pinus* species. These Administration plantations are now being supplemented by extensive plantings by Local Government Councils and other private groups aimed at supplying areas such as the Highlands where timber is scarce. *Casuarina spp.* and fast-growing Eucalypts are generally used to supply round timbers for housing, fences, etc., with the residue being used for fuel.

The Territory of Papua and New Guinea covers a total land area of some 115,000,000 acres of which an estimated 80,400,000 acres are forested. On the accompanying map, the country is divided into four categories defined as follows:

Forest area of known potential (7,000,000 acres). This category includes areas which have been assessed by field survey. The extent, volume and species composition of the forest, together with details of access and infrastructure requirements have been recorded and mapped to a level sufficient for preliminary developmental planning.

Forest area of possible potential (14,000,000 acres). Only limited information is available in these areas. They have been delineated mainly

* Department of Forests, Territory of Papua and New Guinea.

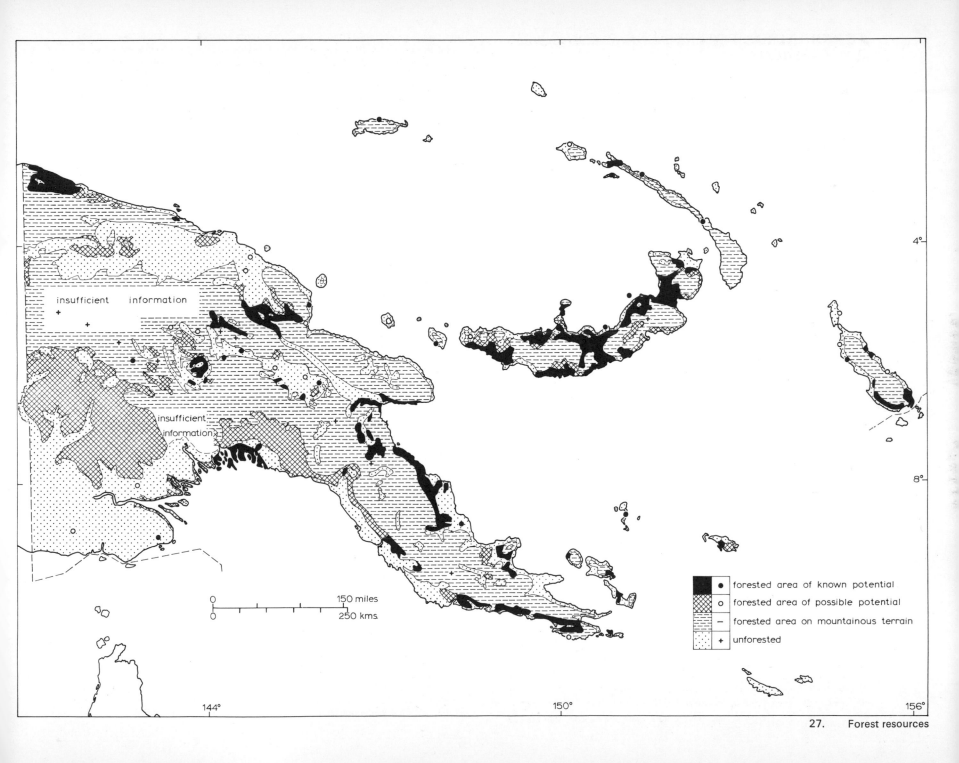

insufficient   information

+

insufficient
information

0   150 miles
0   250 kms.

		forested area of known potential
	o	forested area of possible potential
	—	forested area on mountainous terrain
	+	unforested

27.   Forest resources

AGRICULTURAL POTENTIAL   *F. P. ALAND and D. A. TORLACH* *

but there do not appear to be any prospects for any large scale agricultural development. This classification does not take into account altitude, climatic or edaphic restrictions and consequently presents an overgeneralized picture of the potential of the Territory. For example, along the coast in the Central District the dry climate and infertile soils restrict land usage in practice to predominantly grazing although on Map 28 large areas are shown as being topographically suitable for agriculture.

Land topographically suitable for agriculture embraces arable land, land suitable for permanent tree crops, land suitable for mixed farming and land supporting or capable of supporting limited cash cropping within a predominantly subsistence system (e.g. pyrethrum). A much broader scale of topographical classification can be used in the wet tropics than is normal in temperate lands. Tree crops such as cocoa and coconuts can be planted on very steeply sloping land and erosion is no real problem once the trees are established or a good cover is established. The major limitations are usually problems of access, management and harvesting, not erosion.

The areas of greatest agricultural potential are around the lower aprons and ash derived plains of Recent and Pleistocene volvanoes, the valleys of the Waghi and Markham Rivers and some coastal areas. The largest areas of ash derived plains occur on New Britain, namely the Gazelle Peninsula northeast of the Bainings Mountains, the area from Open Bay to just west of the Willaumez Peninsula and from Rein Bay to Cape Bushing at the western end of the island. These areas in New Britain have the greatest agricultural potential of any one district in the Territory. The Markham Valley consists of predominantly juvenile sands and silts derived from alluvium with minor areas of black earths. The Highlands Highway passes through the Valley giving good year-round access so this area is well suited to grazing, and the production of sorghum, peanuts and dryland rice could also be undertaken. In the Wagni Valley peat soils occur and considerable drainage is required. However, once drained it has been found that the soil potential of this area is considerably higher than was previously believed and tea and coffee are important crops. The coastal belts of New Ireland have soils developed from raised coral beds which are suited to lowland crops although fertilizer or green manuring may be required. Bougainville also has some soils developed on raised coral but vulcanism has added to the fertility of most of the island. The volcanic soils are the most important agricultural soils. The Papuan coastline from Milne Bay to the Gulf of Papua and parts of the Ramu-Markham Valleys are characterized by soils with a high base saturation which restricts the choice of crops grown and the lower Ramu, Gogol and Musa Rivers are subjected to seasonal flooding. The Sepik grasslands suffer from inherently low soil fertility and poor drainage and any development would be costly or impractical especially in the many areas where pot holes are common. The south coast of New Britain has predominantly shallow limestone soils and the rainfall is very high. On the map Western District appears to have considerable potential : topographically this is so but much of this land experiences severe inundation during the wet season and drought during the dry. Also there are problems of poor soil fertility and difficult access. Taking these factors into account Western District is the district of lowest potential. The areas of grazing land of highest potential are the Markham-Ramu Valleys, the lacustrine basins of the Baiyer and Jimi Rivers, the upland valleys and grassy slopes in the Morobe and the highland districts and the more broken topography in the Northern and Central Districts.

Only one per cent of the Territory is first class agricultural land ; 24 per cent is topographically suitable for agriculture but has varying limitations ; four per cent is suitable for grazing ; 55 per cent is deemed unsuitable for any commercial agricultural development and 16 per cent is not categorized because no reliable data are available but it appears to have very little potential.

The agricultural potential map has been restricted through limitations of scale to three classes : land topographically suitable for agriculture, land suitable for grazing, and land which is either unsuitable for commercial agriculture and grazing or for which there is insufficient data available to put into any category (based on information available at 30th June, 1969). Areas in the last category do support a scattered indigenous population practising subsistence agriculture

* Land Utilization Officers, Department of Agriculture, Stock and Fisheries, Port Moresby.

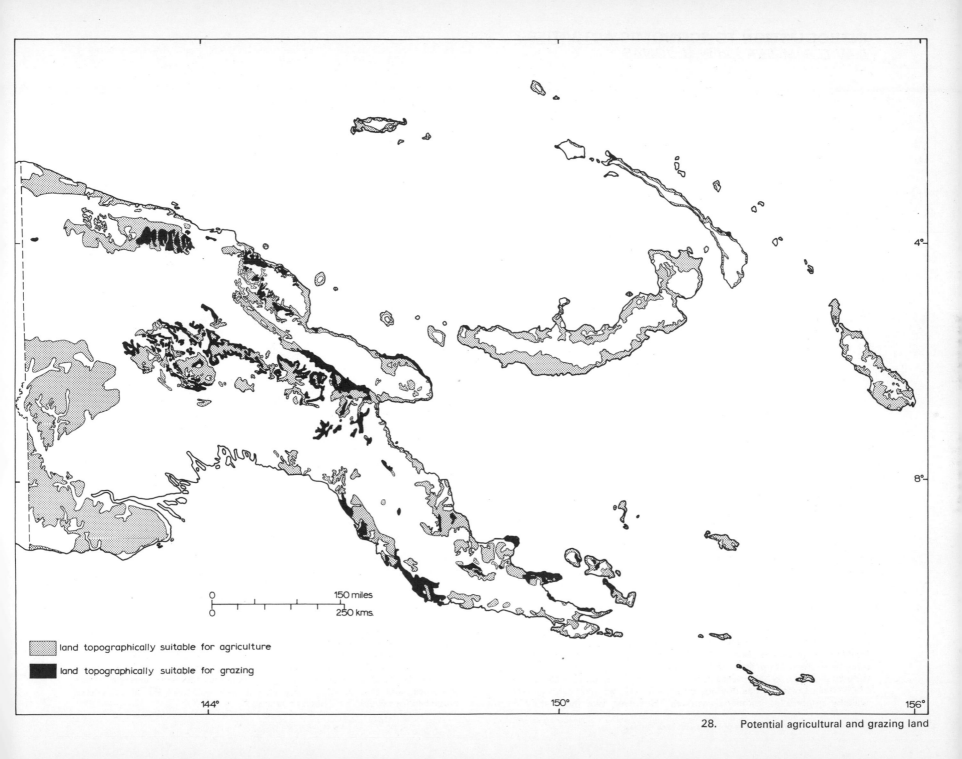

0 _____ 150 miles
0 _____ 250 kms.

land topographically suitable for agriculture

land topographically suitable for grazing

28.   Potential agricultural and grazing land

INTRODUCTION TO ECONOMIC ACTIVITIES
DAVID A. M. LEA and W. J. JONAS *

The indigenous sector of the economy of Papua and New Guinea is mainly concerned with subsistence activities (Map 7). Although most of the maps in this section of the *Atlas* show commercial and non-traditional activities it should not be construed that subsistence activities are not 'economic' but rather that we are limited by lack of adequate information and cannot show many significant distributions and trends. Often the only reliable figures available are for commercial enterprises, many of which are in the hands of expatriates.

Agriculture is the most important element in both the subsistence and commercial sectors of the economy and Map 29 shows the broad categories of land use on non-indigenous rural holdings. There has been little change in plantations over the past few years and crop production has not greatly increased. The most interesting changes are the comparatively new interest in beef cattle and the planting of nuclear estates in the Hoskins and Mount Hagen areas. Maps 30 and 31 are compiled from rather dubious sources but are the first serious attempt to show the regional variations in staple foods of the indigenous population. The next maps, of cash crop production, show the four main export crops and also the relative contributions of indigenous and expatriate communities. In that agriculture is seen as the main road to economic viability in Papua and New Guinea, these maps are very relevant to discussion on indigenization of economic activity. In the past most commercial agriculture has been concentrated in the hands of relatively few, large, foreign-owned companies. Most indigenous cash crops have been grown on land held under traditional land tenure systems. However, the Administration is using agricultural resettlement as a means of encouraging indigenous participation under individual land tenure (Map 33) but as most resettlement schemes are fairly new they are making little contribution to the export economy at present. Industrial activity is of growing importance but is difficult to map because the 1966 Census material has obvious errors, such as including sago workers and wallaby trappers as 'industrial workers'. However, two maps showing the number and size of factories (by numbers employed) and timber industries, have been included. Maps 36 to 39 are of trade and transport. Maps 36 a and b are particularly significant because, related to Maps 5, 7 and 32, regional specialization and district inequalities are apparent, as are changing patterns of the trade of each port as new resources are developed and the road systems spread and interconnect. No map can give sufficient emphasis to the role played by aircraft in the development of Papua and New Guinea—not only in terms of the number of passengers carried and the tons of freight moved but in opening up the interior and in the servicing of inland centres and out-stations. The large imbalance between imports and exports can only be continued while the Australian Government provides some services and the annual grant. At present the grant provides approximately 57 per cent of the total Administration receipts of $153,000,000. This helps to alleviate the shortage of capital and capital assets, which is a characteristic of all developing countries. Public authorities have until very recently provided well over 50 per cent of the gross domestic capital formation but private capital formation is now rapidly increasing.

The last two maps in this group show the distribution of electric power generators and the loans made by the Papua and New Guinea Development Bank. Because the Bank has been operating only for several years it is to be expected that the pattern of lending will show great changes within the next few years, especially since, unlike all other banking institutions in Papua and New Guinea, it is not governed by Australian banking legislation and practice.

As this section reveals, there is a general lack of information on the country's resources. This and the absence of a well developed transport system are two of the greatest barriers to rapid economic development. It is hoped however, with public and private investigations taking place, that sufficient knowledge will soon be available for more detailed assessments of mineral, water and other resources, and that transport surveys will have reached the stage where proposals for development become reality.

* Lecturer in Geography, University of Papua and New Guinea.

LAND USE ON AGRICULTURAL HOLDINGS
D. A. M. LEA

About 96·7 per cent of the land in Papua and New Guinea is held and oper: by indigenes under traditional land tenure systems. The remainder is ei freehold land (0·5 per cent of the total land area), mainly in the Trust Territo or Administration land (2·8 per cent). Nearly all the freehold land was alienate before 1914 although some indigenes have acquired land, particularly in the Northern District of Papua, in fee simple under the *Land (Tenure Conversion) Ordinance* 1963–1967. The Administration land has been inherited from either the earlier German or English administrations or has been purchased or acquired. The forms of non-indigenous tenure are illustrated in the following table:

	Papua (acres)	New Guinea (acres)	Papua and New Guinea (acres)
Freehold land owned by ex-patriates	24,270	516,356	540,626
Freehold under Land Tenure Conversion	4,446	494	4,940
Administration land			
Leased	388,143	441,063	829,206
Native Reserves	67,288	26,804	94,092
Other	1,443,876	865,658	2,309,534

Of the leased Administration land 90·5 per cent has been leased for agricultural, dairying and pastoral purposes—this and the freehold land accounts for the 1,024,691 acres of non-indigenous rural holdings which is only 1·11 per cent of the total land area of Papua and New Guinea. The Administration operates 8·3 per cent of the leased land itself mainly as research stations, experimental and extension stations, the missions hold 8·3 per cent and commercial operators hold the remainder. Of the alienated land, missions own 33·9 per cent and commercial operators the balance.

On these commercial holdings 270,176 acres were planted with coconuts, 121,160 acres with cocoa (often interplanted with coconuts), 14,817 acres with coffee and 35,818 acres were under rubber in 1968. About 20,000 acres are under other crops such as peanuts, tea, fodder crops and vegetables. Map 32 shows how important plantation production is in terms of total Territory production in the four main crops but indigenous participation is growing. Many plantations also have livestock and in 1968 52,621 cattle were grazed on coconut plantations and on some 200,000 acres of pasture—most of it natural.

In 1968 45 per cent of expatriate controlled land was unused. As at least one quarter of this unused land is good agricultural land and often occurs in densely populated areas, a good case can be made that the Administration should enforce development clauses to ensure that usable land is brought into production.

Bibliography:

Bureau of Statistics, 1968. *Rural Industries,* Bulletin No. 9, Konedobu.

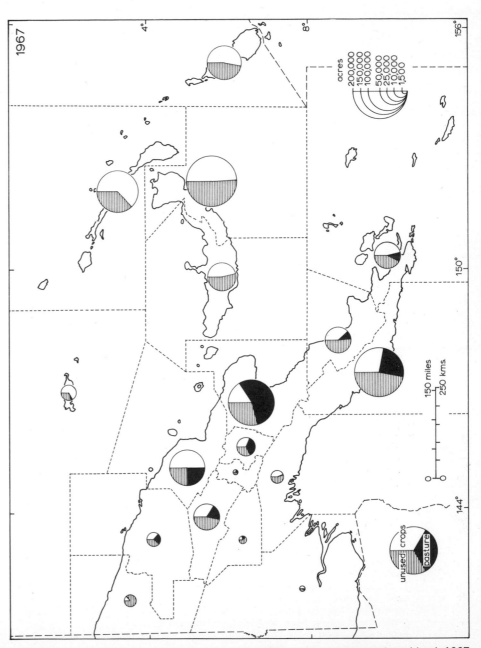

29.   Use of alienated rural land, 1967

STAPLE CROPS AND MAIN SOURCES OF FOOD
D. A. M. LEA

East Sepik District and in the small island groups, the main source of food is starchy root crops grown in gardens, or bananas, or sago. Although each of the staples discussed here may have only one or several botanical names, indigenous farmers can usually identify scores of botanically stable varieties.

Taro. Taro is the collective name for lily-like plants belonging to the family Araceae. The main edible taro is *Colocasia esculenta* although *Xanthosoma* spp. or 'taro kong kong' as it is known in Pidgin, is becoming more important in the lowland areas. Taros thrive in shady, moist places and are propagated by planting cuttings from the top of the corm or small axillary buds. Among some groups such as the Baruya and the Karam, taro is irrigated.

Yams. The most important yam species are *Dioscorea alata* and *D. esculenta*. Yams are propagated by planting small tubers or sections of tubers and usually a system of supports is provided for the vine. Yams flourish best in areas with a deep well-drained soil and a definite dry season. The seasonality of the crop often results in periods of seasonal shortage but yams have the advantage of being the only tropical root crop which can be stored for periods of up to six months. In some areas such as the Maprik Sub-District and the Trobriand Islands, giant ceremonial yams up to 12 feet long are frequently grown.

Sweet Potato (*Ipomoea batatas*). Sweet potato ('kau kau' in Pidgin) is the main staple of the Highlands but is also important in many coastal areas. It is propagated by planting leafy shoots, and matures in 4–18 months. As the crop will not keep, only a few tubers are removed at the time and each plant can continue bearing for several months. Sweet potato is sensitive to wet soil, drought and frost but the range of tolerance is wide and it will grow in both humid coastal areas and at altitudes of up to 8,500 ft.

Bananas (*Musa spp.*). Bananas are the most ubiquitous crop in New Guinea but in the Markham Valley and around Port Moresby they are the staple food. Grown both in gardens and semi-perennial stands, banana varieties can be divided into two main groups—those which can be eaten cooked and those which are sweet and can be eaten fresh.

Sago (*Metroxylon sagu*). The sago palms grow either in natural stands or are planted from shoots in shallow fresh-water swampy areas. Each palm takes 8–15 years to mature and the pith in the trunk contains starch which is laboriously extracted by pounding the pith, filtering the sago flour from woody fibres and collecting the starch by sedimentation. Sago starch can be preserved and stored for several months and was often an important item in traditional trading systems. It has a high calorific content but contains virtually no protein or vitamins. In areas where it is the staple food the diet is supplemented by protein-rich foods from lake or river and by fresh fruits or vegetables from small levee gardens. In many areas sago is either a supplementary food or used as a famine food to overcome seasonal shortage of garden crops.

In some areas, especially around the towns, traditional staples are being replaced by trade-store foods and by the easily grown and high yielding cassava (*Manihot esculenta*). Hundreds of other foods are available from forest, grassland, planted trees, lakes, rivers and sea. It is not unusual for an individual garden to contain 20–30 different species of food plant with many different varieties of the main food crops.

Other supplementary foods which are almost ubiquitous or near staples in some localities include sugar cane (*Saccharum officinarum*), corn (*9ea mays*), and 'pit pit' (*Saccharum edule*) in the lowlands and the potato (*Solarum tuberosum*) in the Highlands. Many tree crops are important, especially the coconut (*Cocos nucifera*) and the breadfruit (*Artocarpus spp.*).

Bibliography:

Barrau, J., 1958. *Subsistence Agriculture in Melanesia*, Honolulu.

Massal, E., and Barrau, J., 1956. *Food Plants of the South Sea Islands*, Noumea.

The data for this map and for the following map of crop combinations was compiled from the stratification cards used to collect preliminary data for the 1966 Census. On these cards administrative officers were asked to show for each Census Division *inter alia* the approximate percentage of total food production obtained from the major food crops or other staples. This map shows the most important source of food in each area.

Except for hunting in the Star Mountains and fishing in the Murik Lakes of the

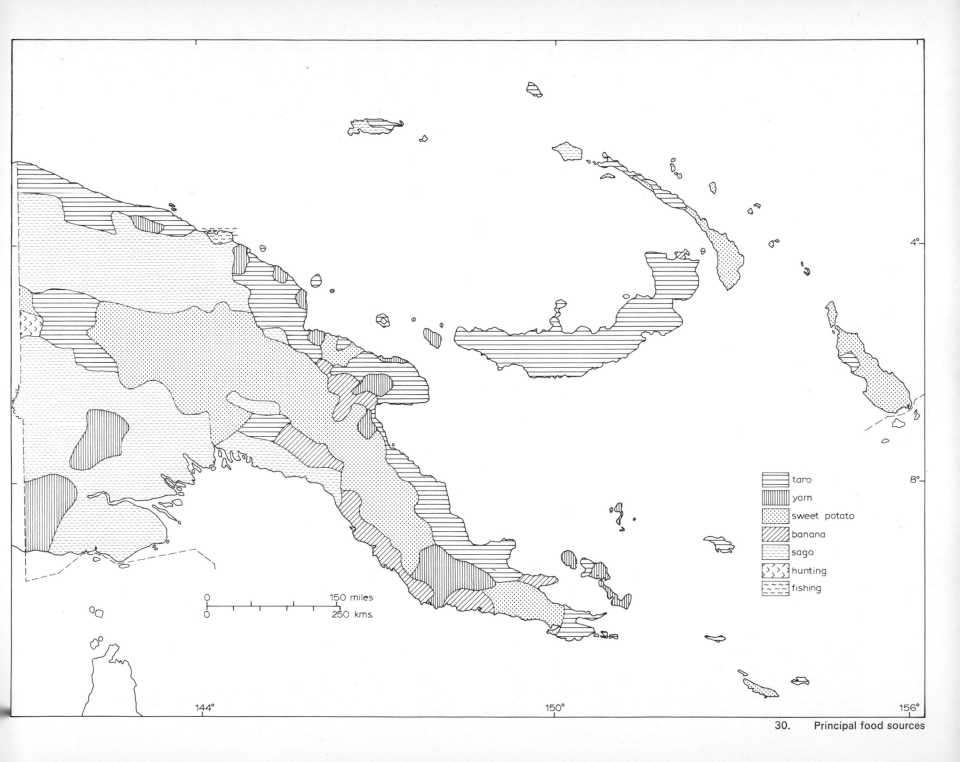

▤	taro
▥	yam
⣿	sweet potato
▨	banana
⣿	sago
⧓	hunting
≈	fishing

0   150 miles
0   250 kms.

30.   Principal food sources

CROP COMBINATIONS *D. A. M. LEA and R. GERARD WARD*

Crop or food source combinations have been calculated by the method devised by Weaver (1954) and modified by Thomas (1963). Estimates for each Census Division of the percentage of total sustenance provided by different crops or food sources are given in the 1966 Census Stratification Cards and this has been used as the basic source of data. The main weakness of the data is that all the many minor sources of food have been ignored so that on the stratification cards 100 per cent of food may be shown as coming from one to four staples whereas minor foods are important for social and dietary reasons in all areas. Ten food sources are considered: taro, yams, bananas, sweet potato, sago, rice, coconuts, hunting, marine products and 'others'.

The last of these consists principally of purchased food (other than rice) and minor crops such as cassava, other vegetables, wild foods and traded food. The actual percentage in each Census Division is compared with the theoretical distribution if all food sources represented therein were equally important. Food sources "are ranked in order of descending magnitude and the differences between the actual and theoretical percentages calculated, beginning with monoculture, in which one crop (food source) accounts for 100% and proceeding from 2-crop combination (each crop 50%) through progressively larger combinations to find the best fit. This is determined by the method of least squares" (Coppock, 1964, pp. 211–212). An example of a theoretical three-crop combination would be taro 33·3 per cent; yams 33·3 per cent; sago 33·3 per cent with all other crops absent. On Map 31 different shadings indicate whether an area has a one-two-three-four or more crop combination, and the actual crops concerned are shown in rank order by letter symbols, e.g. TYS represents a three-crop combination with taro (first crop), yams (second crop) and sago (third crop). High combinations indicate greater variety of staples but not necessarily a better diet since much of the protein and vitamin content of the diet is obtained from non-staple foods such as leaves, vegetables, fruits and nuts. The omission of a crop does not imply that it is entirely absent from an area but merely that it is not sufficiently important to appear in the combination. It should also be noted that many Census Divisions cover a wide range of environments and there is inevitably a considerable amount of generalization. Within most Census Divisions there will be areas whose crop patterns do not conform to the dominant combination of the Division.

In most of the Highlands, the sweet potato is the overwhelmingly dominant crop. In some individual valleys, taro may become dominant but in most areas this is of relatively minor importance. One-crop combinations also occur in the sago-growing areas of Gulf District, in the Lake Kutubu area and along the border between Chimbu and Gulf Districts. In central New Britain taro dominates while in much of Bougainville the sweet potato has displaced taro as the one-crop combination in recent years. This is due to devastation of the taro crop by insect pests. The same process is occurring in parts of New Britain. In lowland areas, particularly the lowland portions of Morobe and Madang districts and the coastal areas of southeastern Papua, more complex crop combinations occur with considerable local variety in the rank order of particular crops. This is due mainly to the lowland areas having an environment in which most of the staples grow readily, but it is also a reflection of European contact breaking down traditional and often ceremonial dominance of one crop.

The reliability of the data on which this map is based is not high and therefore the map should only be considered as a first approximation. Nevertheless, it does indicate that although individual gardens may contain many different plants and although there is a wide variety of foods available in the sea, rivers and forests, the diet of most Papuans and New Guineans is usually dominated by one to three starchy staples which are vegetatively propagated. The first crop, or main staple (as shown on Map 30) is usually that which is best suited ecologically for the particular environment. Beyond this it is difficult to make any generalization, except that sweet potato is obviously becoming more important at the expense of yams and taro, and that we expect a number of changes and more high-combination crops as more detailed information comes to hand.

Bibliography:

Coppock, J. T., 1964. *Agricultural Atlas of England and Wales,* London.
Thomas, D., 1963. *Agriculture in Wales during the Napoleonic Wars: a Study in the geographical interpretation of historical sources,* Cardiff.
Weaver, J. C., 1954. 'Crop-combination regions in the Middle West', *Geographical Review,* Vol. 44, pp. 560–572.

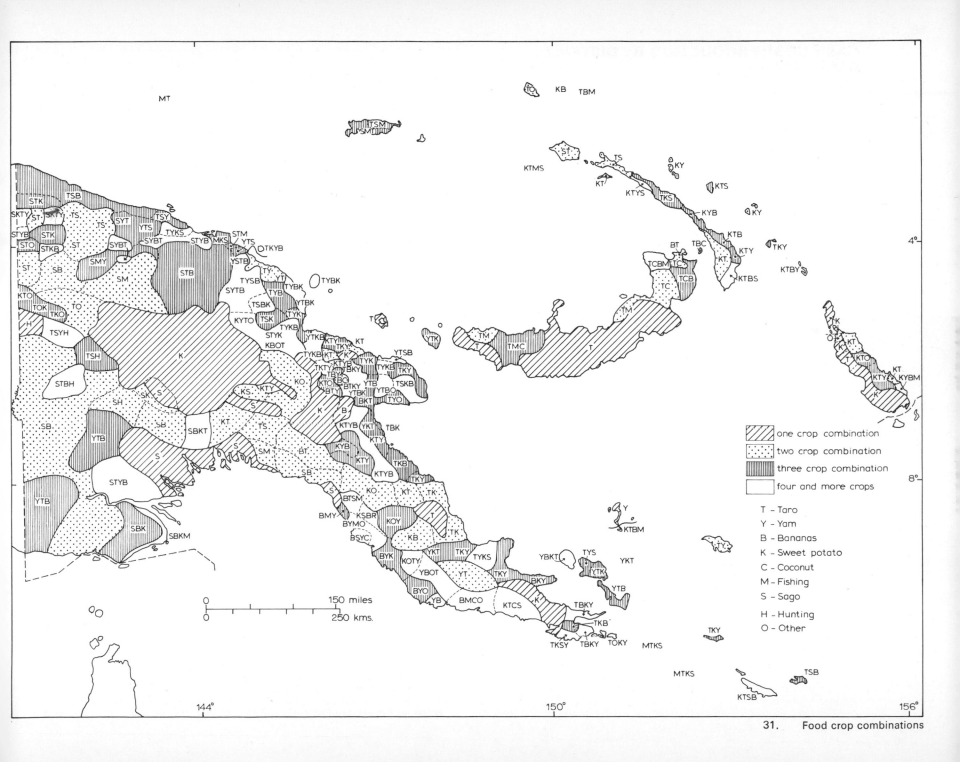

MT

KB   TBM

TSM
SMT

ST
KTMS

TS   KY
KT   KTS
KTYS   TKS
KYB   KY

STK   TSB   BT   TBC   KTB
SKTY ST SKTY TS.   TSY   STM   TCBM TCS   KTY   TKY
STYB   STK   SYT   YTS   YTS   TCB   KT.
STO   STKB   ST   SYBT SYBT TYKS STYB MKS YTS   TC   KTBS   KTBY
ST   SMY   SYTB   OTKYB   4°
SB   SM   STB   YSTB
                                                              TY.   TYBK   TYBK
KTO   TYSB YT   TM   TM
TOK TKO   TO   SYTB   TYB YTBK   TMC   T
H   TSBK   YTBK   T
TSYH   KYTO TSK TYKB   TMC   T
TSH   STYK TYKB   TYK
                    K   KBOT   YTKB KTY KT
STBH   TKTY TKY. KT   YTSB
                                        KS KTY KO. TBY BKY   TYKB TKY
        SH   S   KTOR BTKY YTB   TYKB
SB.   S   BT BTKY YTBO TSKB
        SBKT   K   B   BKT   TYO
SB   YTB   SB   K
                        S   KT   TS   KTYB YKT TBK
                                                          KYB   KTY
YTB   STYB   S   SM   KTY
                                            BT   KTYB
        SBK SBKM   S   BTSM KO   TKB
                                        BMY KSBR KT TK   TKY
YTB   BYMO KOY   T   TBK
                                        BSYC   TK KTY
                        SBK   KB
                                        BYK KOTY YKT TKY TYKS
                                            YBOT YT   TKY
                                            BYO YB BMCO KTCS K
                                                              TBKY
                                                  TKB
                                        TKSY TBKY TOKY   MTKS

        150 miles
        250 kms.

TO
KB
ST

KTBM
Y
KTBM

TY
YBKT
TYS   YKT
YTK
YTB
TKY

MTKS   TSB
        KTSB

one crop combination
two crop combination
three crop combination
four and more crops

T – Taro
Y – Yam
B – Bananas
K – Sweet potato
C – Coconut
M – Fishing
S – Sago
H – Hunting
O – Other

8°

TKY
KTO
KT
KT
KTY KYBM
K

31.   Food crop combinations

144°   150°   156°

CASH CROP PRODUCTION BY DISTRICT
D. A. M. LEA

Within the cash economy, primary production is the major element and in 1965–66 accounted for 36·9 per cent of the monetary-sector production of the gross Territory Product. Primary production is also the main source of foreign exchange. In 1967–68 exports of coconut products ($21,000,000), coffee ($14,000,000), cocoa ($12,000,000) and rubber ($2,000,000) provided 84 per cent of total export income.

Commercial agriculture has two main forms: expatriate plantation production of perennial tree crops for export; and smallholder indigenous production, either concentrating on dual-purpose crops which can be eaten or sold (e.g. coconuts or surplus vegetables) or on exotic tree crops grown for the export trade but under traditional land tenure systems.

Plantation agriculture began in the 1880s when the Germans established coconut plantations in the Bismarck Archipelago and on the mainland of New Guinea, especially along the Madang and Finschhafen coast. In spite of setbacks in the depression of the 1930s and during World War II, the expansion of the market economy until the 1950s was almost entirely the result of the establishment of expatriate mining enterprises and coconut plantations. Since the 1950s many coffee plantations have been established in the Highlands and cocoa has been planted either as a sole crop or interplanted in coconut plantations. In 1967 there were 1,236 holdings, 185 operated by the Administration and 349 operated by Missions. In all, these holdings totalled 1,026,791 acres and employed 53,146 persons. As there are only 315 owners, lessees and share farmers it is likely that there are many combined operations. Except for coffee, plantations produce the major share of the main export crops.

The growing of indigenous cash crops is a comparatively recent development in Papua and New Guinea. Before World War II there were a number of attempts to encourage indigenous commercial agriculture but these schemes, nearly all based on some form of compulsion, floundered on problems of land tenure, work organization, motivation or income distribution. In 1938–39, £1,000,000 was earned from agricultural exports but less than a quarter of the total export production came from village farmers who, on the whole, collected coconuts and prepared copra when cash was needed for a specific purpose.

Since World War II, and particularly since 1956, there has been a considerable diversification of production and indigenes have been making an increasing contribution to commercial farm production. In 1968 indigenous farmers produced just over 30 per cent of the copra, 67 per cent of the coffee and 24 per cent of the cocoa. Rubber remains an expatriate plantation crop and indigenous production is only 0·23 per cent of total production.

Two major new crops, oil palm and tea, have been established in West New Britain and in the Western Highlands but, with the initial emphasis on the 'Nuclear Estate', main production will remain in expatriate hands for a number of years. The current Five Year Plan estimates that by 1972–73 only 300 tons of a total tea crop of 3,100 tons will be produced by indigenes; and of a total palm oil and oil kernel production of 5,100 tons only 1,100 tons will be produced by indigenes.

In 1968, nearly $6,000,000 was spent on imported rice, $1,300,000 on imported sugar and $1,000,000 on imported fresh vegetables. All these crops have great potential as import replacement crops and could provide local employment as well as saving foreign exchange. Pyrethrum and passion-fruit, two cash crops grown in the Highlands, both have a probable maximum market of about 800 tons within the next few years.

It is intended that there should be a beef-cattle herd of about 300,000 by 1980 but in 1968 there were only 56,600 head, mostly concentrated on non-indigenous cattle leases in the Markham, Ramu and tributary valleys. In 1968 only 4,600 cattle were indigenously owned.

Map 31 shows great regional specialization of crops. About half of the coconut acreage and production is in New Britain, New Ireland and Bougainville and three-quarters of the cocoa is in the same three Districts. About 90 per cent of Papua and New Guinea's coffee is Arabica type, grown between 3,000 and 6,500 feet, so most of the production is concentrated in the Western Highlands, Chimbu and Eastern Highlands Districts with a smaller concentration in the Wau Valley of the Morobe District. Robusta type coffee is grown in the coastal areas, particularly in the East Sepik District. In the face of world coffee marketing problems there is no planned expansion of the coffee industry but it is anticipated that production will rise to 20,000 tons within the next five years. Nearly all rubber is grown in Papua and 81 per cent is grown in the Central District.

References:

Bureau of Statistics, 1967. Port Moresby, *Rural Industries,* Bulletin No. 9.

Department of Agriculture, Stock and Fisheries, 1969. *Crop Statistics* (Indigenous), *1967–68,* Port Moresby.

Territory of Papua and New Guinea, 1968. *Programmes and Policies of the Economic Development of Papua and New Guinea,* Port Moresby.

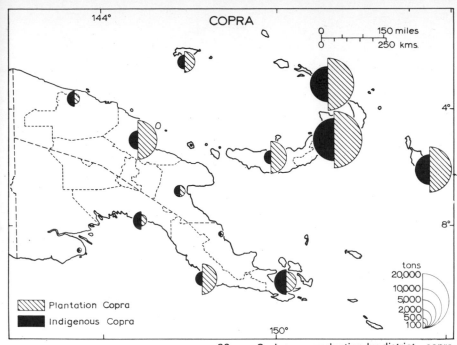

COPRA

Plantation Copra
Indigenous Copra

tons
20,000
10,000
5,000
2,000
500
100

32a.   Cash crop production by district—copra

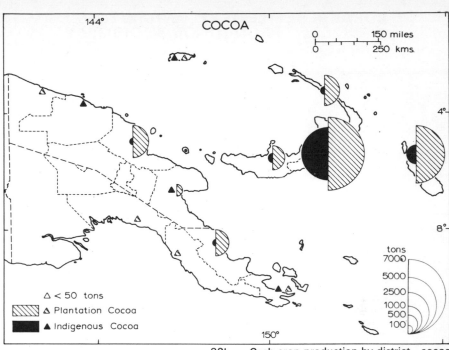

COCOA

△ < 50 tons
△ Plantation Cocoa
▲ Indigenous Cocoa

tons
7000
5000
2500
1000
500
100

32b.   Cash crop production by district—cocoa

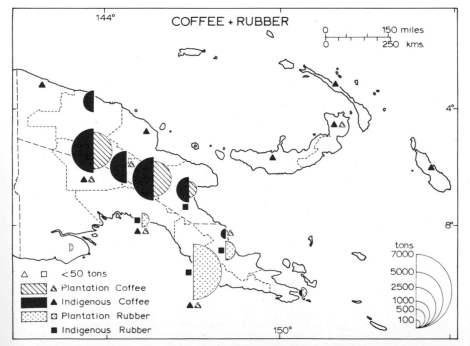

COFFEE + RUBBER

△ □ < 50 tons
△ Plantation Coffee
▲ Indigenous Coffee
⊡ Plantation Rubber
■ Indigenous Rubber

tons
7000
5000
2500
1000
500
100

32c.   Cash crop production by district—coffee and rubber

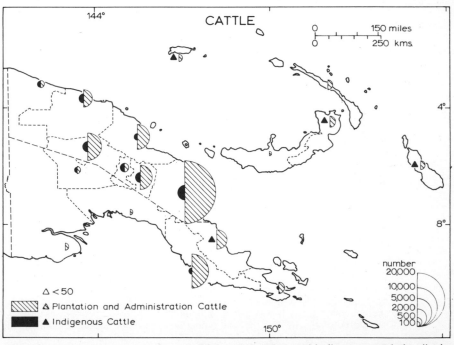

CATTLE

△ < 50
△ Plantation and Administration Cattle
▲ Indigenous Cattle

number
20,000
10,000
5,000
2,000
500
100

32d.   Plantation and indigenous cattle by district

RURAL RESETTLEMENT *ANTON PLOEG* *

'Rural resettlement' is the allocation of land to individual Papuans and New Guineans for commercial farming. This policy, first implemented in 1952 in Papua and New Guinea, has undergone important changes and further changes may occur. Initially blocks were made available by local government councils. These schemes comprised about 2,200 acres and were unsuccessful (Cheetham, 1962–63 : 71). Since 1959 the allocation of blocks has been managed by the central administration. Map 33 deals only with the latter schemes. Groups of blocks occupy continuous stretches of land, called settlements. Contiguous settlements are jointly represented on the map by a single symbol.

Rural resettlement serves several purposes. Firstly, it should boost indigenous agricultural production, and secondly, it facilitates provision of agricultural extension services. Blocks are held on individual tenure, and this promotes the establishment of a new system of land tenure along Australian lines. This is considered advantageous since indigenous land tenure systems are varied and have communal features which may oblige individual cash croppers to share yields from their crops with less industrious co-holders. Furthermore, until recently, land under traditional tenure was not accepted as security for loans.

The Department of Lands advertises the availability of land, hears applications and selects the settlers to whom blocks are leased. The Department of Agriculture provides extension services while road construction and school establishment are organized by the Department of Public Works and Education respectively. Most block holders need credit to finance the development of their blocks. Initially this was provided by the Ex-servicemen's Credit Board (which only lent to ex-servicemen settlers from 1958 to 1962) and the Native Loans Board. In 1967 a Project Planning Team was established to improve co-ordination between various departments, and between departments and loan bodies. Following a recommendation of the International Bank for Reconstruction and Development (1965 : 378–85), a full-time specialist agency, the Papua and New Guinea Development Bank, was established and in 1969 took over the operations of the Credit and Loans Boards. Development loans provide a monthly cash allowance, usually of $8, while other components of the loan, such as tools and planting materials, are either given in kind or the holder receive purchase orders to buy them. This aspect of the scheme is greatly resented by many settlers. Until 1969, loans did not contain a component to pay the wages of labourers. This follows the policy that blocks should be of such a size that the holder and the other members of his family can develop it by their own labour. The Development Bank is now considering decreasing the size of the cash allowance and providing money for the clearing of blocks by labourers to facilitate the task of the block holder, and speed up the clearing and probably the development of the blocks.

Annual returns from blocks vary greatly, depending upon the principal crop and current prices. Many coconut blocks, for example, are of about 25 acres and when fully planted with mature coconut palms may yield 6 to 12 tons of copra annually. At 1969 prices this means an annual gross income of $750 to $1,500 whereas a 15-acre oil palm block would yield about $3,000 annually. Rural resettlement is expensive. It has been estimated (Guise 1967 : Appendix C) that development costs as much as $10,000 per block. Moreover, the policy has suffered several setbacks. Firstly, because of lack of co-ordination between the bodies concerned with resettlement, several settlements lack or have lacked basic facilities such as schools and reasonable accessibility. Long delays in granting loans made holders reluctant to settle on their blocks and start development. Secondly, some areas used for settlements were unsuitable for the recommended cash crop. Finally, on some settlements crops have been severely damaged by diseases and insects. As a result of these setbacks and the recent introduction of the policy, resettlement has contributed little to the national economy to date and much of the land allocated has not yet been brought under cultivation.

The resettlement programme initially fell short of its target. By early 1968 about 2,500 blocks comprising almost 60,000 acres had been made available, whereas it had been planned to have 7,500 blocks by 1967. However, during the first two years of the present five-year plan which began in mid-1968, about 20,000 acres were allocated. This is more than half of the total area to be allocated during the whole period covered by the plan (P.N.G., 1968 : 20).

Bibliography:

Cheetham, R. J., 1962–63. 'The Development of Indigenous Agriculture, Land Settlement and Rural Credit Facilities in Papua and New Guinea', *The Papua and New Guinea Agricultural Journal,* Vol. 15, pp. 67–78.

Guise, J., 1967. *Minority Report by John Guise, M.H.A. Milne Bay Open Electorate, of the Parliamentary Mission's Visit to Malaysia to Examine Land Resettlement Schemes;* Cyclostyled.

International Bank for Reconstruction and Development, 1965. *The Economic Development of the Territory of Papua and New Guinea,* Baltimore.

Territory of Papua and New Guinea (T.P.N.G.), 1968. *Programmes and Policies for the Economic Development of Papua and New Guinea,* Port Moresby.

* Research Fellow, New Guinea Research Unit, Australian National University.

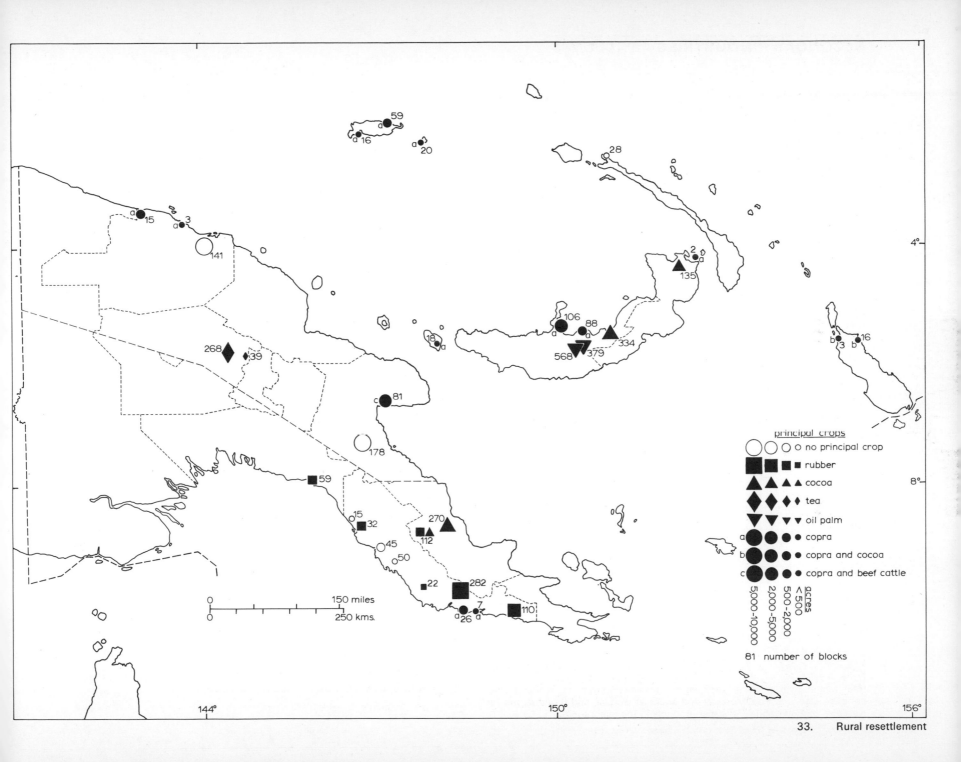

principal crops

○○○ no principal crop

■■■ rubber

▲▲▲ cocoa

◆◆◆ tea

▼▼▼ oil palm

a ●●● copra

b ●●● copra and cocoa

c ●●● copra and beef cattle

acres
5,000–10,000
2,000–5,000
500–2,000
< 500

81 number of blocks

33. Rural resettlement

SECONDARY INDUSTRIES *W. J. JONAS*

For the collection and preparation of the statistics on which the map of factories is based, a factory is defined as "any establishment engaged in manufacturing, repairing, assembling, preparing, treating or making up any other article or substance and in which four or more persons are engaged or where power (other than manual) is used". The factories can be classified on the basis of size or according to the nature of their produce. In the latter case four broad categories are recognized :

(a) Industrial Metals, Machines and Conveyances
(b) Food, Drink and Tobacco
(c) Sawmills, Joinery and Plywood
(d) Miscellaneous

Most of the factories (72 per cent) employ less than 20 workers. These small factories are concentrated mainly in the four major urban areas or at the sources of production of those raw materials, such as rubber and cocoa, which are processed. When classified according to type the largest group of factories is concerned with industrial metals, machines and conveyances. This group includes general engineering, ship and boat building, sheet metal and electrical machinery working, aircraft construction and repair and, the single activity which involves the greatest number of factories and the largest body of workers, motor vehicle repairs.

The timber industry ranks high in factory production and employs over 33 per cent of the total factory work-force. More than 20 per cent of the total factory value of output comes from sawmills, plywood mills and joinery workshops, with the plywood and veneer factories of Bulolo and Lae accounting for over half the value of the timber products. Approximately 23 per cent of the factory work-force is concerned with the processing and production of food, drink and tobacco. A large proportion of this work is the processing of plantation crops for eventual consumption abroad. Baking and beverage-production take place in most of the major towns. Port Moresby and Lae each possesses a brewery and public abbatoirs, and twist tobacco and cigarettes are produced in Madang.

These three categories account for over 86 per cent of the total factory work-force. A relatively small number of people are employed in 13 per cent of the total factories to produce such items as cement products, which include concrete blocks at Port Moresby and bricks at Goroka, and furniture and furnishings, printed goods and paper products in the major towns.

The small number of factories catering for 2,184,986 (1966) people, the concentration of factory size in the less-than-20 class, the small proportion of the total work-force employed in factories, and the nature of the factory produce reflect the history and level of economic development and the related resource base on which production must rely. As is typical in underdeveloped countries in the tropics, factory production has long concentrated on the processing of plantation crops for export. In general the processing units have been foreign-owned, small in size and usually located on the plantations. Changes which have occured, while not great in number, are significant because of their departure from the established practice. Included here are the setting up of central processing units (owned by local government councils or co-operatives) at Kundiawa, where coffee is processed, and around Blanche Bay where the Tolai Cocoa Project operates cocoa fermentaries. Larger factories also produce coconut oil and copra oil cake at Rabaul, passion-fruit pulp at Goroka, Mount Hagen and Chimbu, and pyrethrum extract at Mount Hagen. Tea factories are located at Mount Hagen and Garaina, and a crayfish freezing and processing factory operates at Kairuku.

Although they have developed slowly, and then usually at the instigation of Government agencies, Missions or individual expatriates, indigenous factory enterprises are increasing in number and significance. Village or council sawmills operate at Moveave, Lokanu, Paparatava, Laiagam, and Mul-Dei, while Rabaul is the site of an indigenously owned and controlled furniture and joinery factory. The weaving of woollen blankets and garments is now practised at Mendi, Togoba, Goroka, Lufa, Karimui, Tarabo, Wonenara and Kundiawa, all of which are situated in the Highlands. Stabilized earth bricks are manufactured near Kavieng. At Bes Mission near Aitape and along the Purari Delta parts of sago palm leaf sheaf are woven into wall sheets. In all cases, other than wool weaving, these enterprises utilize local raw materials and produce mainly for a local market.

Bibliography:
Bureau of Statistics, *1966–67 Secondary Industries,* Bulletin No. 9, Port Moresby.
Wilson, R. K., and Garnaut, R., 1968. 'A survey of Village Industries in Papua and New Guinea'. *New Guinea Research Unit Bulletin* No. 25.

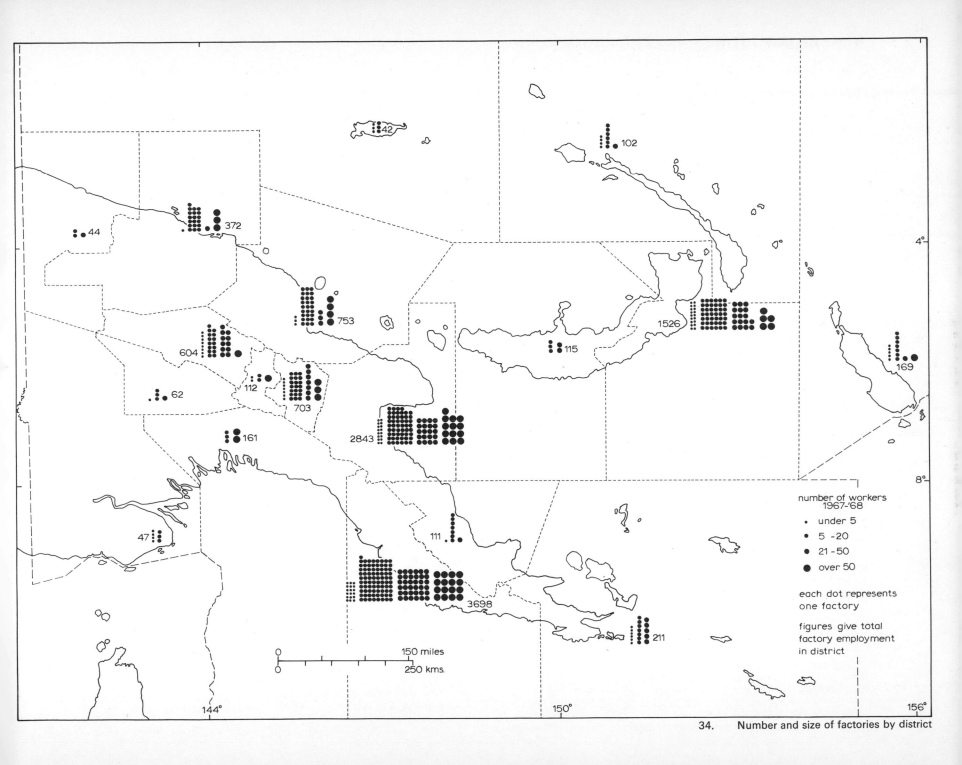

42

102

372

44

753

1526

604

115

112

169

62

703

161

2843

111

47

3698

211

number of workers
1967-'68

· under 5

• 5 -20

● 21 - 50

⬤ over 50

each dot represents
one factory

figures give total
factory employment
in district

0   150 miles

0   250 kms.

4°

8°

144°   150°   156°

34.   Number and size of factories by district

TIMBER INDUSTRIES   *R. KENT WILSON* *

On the mainland the geographical pattern of sawmills has three main linear elements; one along the central Papuan coast, another west from Lae through the highlands, and a third along the north coast. In the outer islands, the sawmills are mainly found on the eastern sides or ends of the islands, the same parts which have historically been the main areas of plantation settlement. The exceptions are the timber export enterprises.

Table 1   *Capacity and ownership of sawmills, by Districts, 1968*

District	Approx. daily log input capacity; one shift (su. ft.)	Private Enterprise	Government Depts.	Mission	Indigenously owned; Co-op or Co.	Total	Average Capacity
Western	1,500	1				1	1,500
Gulf	31,000	3			1	4	8,000
Central	68,000	13		2		15	4,500
Milne Bay	25,000	2		2		4	6,000
Northern	5,000	1				1	5,000
Southern Hlds.	5,100		3			3	1,700
Total Papua	135,600	20	3	4	1	28	
E. Highlands Chimbu	28,000	3		1		4	7,000
W. Highlands	25,000	3		5		8	3,250
W. Sepik	2,000	1				1	2,000
E. Sepik	17,000	2		2		4	4,250
Madang	3,500			2		2	1,750
Morobe	189,000	5			1	6	31,500
E. New Britain	34,500	6			1	7	4,930
W. New Britain	77,000	3		1		4	19,250
New Ireland	2,000	1				1	2,000
Bougainville	12,500	2		1		3	4,100
Manus	1,000	1				1	1,000
Total NG	366,500	27				41	
Total TPNG	502,100	47	3	16	3	69	

Table 1 shows Chimbu as the only district without a mill in 1968, while the mills in the Western District and Manus are very small-capacity units. This table also shows that although most mills, and particularly the larger ones, are owned by private enterprise about one-third are operated by Missions Government Departments and indigenously-owned companies or co-operatives At times Local Government Councils have come to own and operate mills. Three mills now operating (and more in the past) have been set up by village groups who have been helped by some form of supervision or oversight from the Department of Forests, the Co-operative movement or Missions.

The larger towns are the main markets for sawn timber, so that mills have often been located in or near urban areas. However, Port Moresby, Madang and Rabaul are partly supplied with timber along the routes shown by arrows on the map. As mills must generally be located near logging grounds, the separation of some mills from their main markets suggests that there may be a dearth of accessible timber near those towns or that timber areas are difficult to purchase from indigenous owners. In the Gulf and East Sepik districts most mills are located in riverine swamps on the banks of a main river channel, to which logs are generally towed in rafts. The timber is then shipped out by coastal boats to the main markets.

Rather differently the locational criteria of export enterprises have been to tap large timber resources mostly in convenient coastal situations, and located so that large overseas vessels can be loaded, usually at off-shore anchorages. The Bulolo Valley differs from the newer coastal localities. The valley possessed two towns, Wau and Bulolo and a road outlet to Lae before the imminent decline of gold-mining prompted the establishment of a plywood mill at Bulolo. Here above 2,000 ft. (600 metres) parts of the valley sides are covered with *Auracaria* (Hoop and Klinki Pine), a softwood type highly prized for its ease of working and attractive appearance. Off-cuts not used for ply sheets are sawn at an adjacent mill and exported to Australia. Two other mills near Bulolo also export sawn pine to Australia. The plywood enterprise is jointly owned by the gold-mining company and the Commonwealth Government. Originally sales were made on the American and Australian markets, but the American market has been lost to competitors such as Taiwan, Japan and the Philippines. At present the domestic market absorbs a third of the output. In 1966–67 the value of output from sawmills and plywood mills was $8,500,000 and value of production (value added) $4,800,000.. The market for sawn timber is mainly local. The use of imported processed building materials has cut into the local market for sawn timber. It has been difficult to establish markets in either Japan or Australia for the unproven hardwood types which were expected to account for the growth of sawn timber exports.

* Senior Lecturer in Economic Geography, Faculty of Commerce, University of Melbourne.

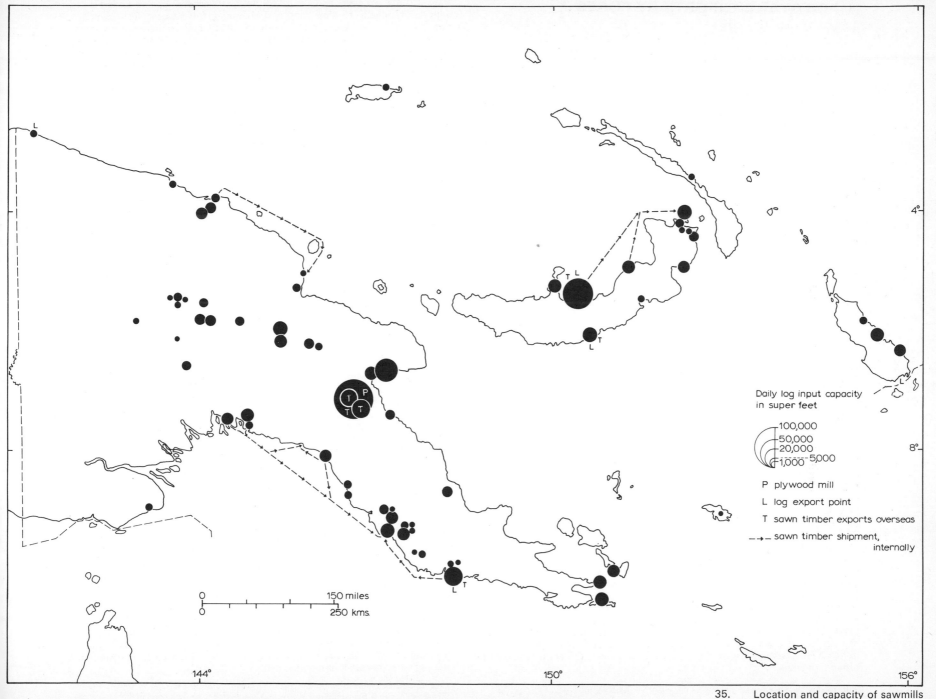

Daily log input capacity
in super feet

100,000
50,000
20,000
5,000
1,000

P plywood mill

L log export point

T sawn timber exports overseas

—→— sawn timber shipment,
        internally

0 ___ 150 miles
0 ___ 250 kms.

4°

8°

144°   150°   156°

35.   Location and capacity of sawmills

IMPORTS AND EXPORTS BY PORTS
MARION W. WARD *

Rabaul (34·7 per cent) and Lae (33·9 per cent) are the leading export ports, with Port Moresby (13·8 per cent) and Madang (10·0 per cent) less important. Virtually all exports are primary products which have undergone only preliminary processing. The exports of each port reflect the economy of its hinterland. Coconut products and cocoa produced in the Gazelle Peninsula and nearby islands are exported through Rabaul. The same products are grown along the Madang coast and are exported through Madang while most of Madang's coffee was flown in from the Highlands. Before the Highlands highway to Lae was opened much larger amounts were handled by Madang. Lae's coffee exports are produced in the Highlands and timber and plywood produced at Bulolo. Copra and rubber (from plantations along the Papuan coast and inland at Sogeri and from indigenous cash-croppers) and fish from the Gulf of Papua are main exports of Port Moresby.

As in most dependent territories, external trade is closely tied to the metropolitan power, in this case Australia, which in 1967–68, supplied 54 per cent of imports and took 42 per cent of exports. The United States supplied 13 per cent of imports and took eight per cent of exports, the United Kingdom five per cent and 29 per cent and Japan supplied 10 per cent of imports. Australia's dominance of total trade has declined from 56 per cent of total trade in 1963–64 to 50 per cent in 1967–68. Over the same period America's share has risen from five to 12 per cent and Japan's from six to nine per cent. The trend is likely to continue.

Port Moresby, Lae, Rabaul and Madang, have dominated overseas trade for several decades. The value of Port Moresby's imports has been from four to six times greater than that of exports throughout the period 1955–56 to 1967–68 and during this time the value of imports has almost quadrupled while that of exports has not quite doubled. Most of these imports are consumed in the town of Port Moresby itself; some are redistributed to other coastal centres by sea (Map 37) while a small proportion is distributed into a primary hinterland which includes virtually all southern Papua.

Rabaul's trade pattern is more balanced. Imports have almost tripled and exports more than doubled in value from 1955–56 to 1967–68. Of all ports Lae has shown the most dramatic growth in the past four years. Since 1965–66 it has been the second port of the country. The opening of the Highlands highway in 1965–66 made Lae the main import port for this developing area and the export port for Highlands coffee. Imports have increased six-fold in this time period and exports four-fold. It is likely that Lae's trade will continue to expand at least until Madang gains road connection to the Highlands. Madang's trade showed a steady increase for 1955–56 to 1965–66, but a marked decline in subsequent years, because of the loss of its Highlands hinterland to Lae. Wewak's imports have increased considerably since 1965–66, probably due to the expansion of the Moem Army base and the subsequent increase in high- and middle-income consumers. The development of road access into the Sepik Valley is likely to stimulate further trade through this port. The trade of Samarai has been more or less stagnant throughout the period under consideration as this port now serves only a limited population in the fragmented Milne Bay district. Kavieng's trade has increased slightly over the same period and, like Rabaul, it is notable that the value of exports, exceeded imports in each year shown. Trade through the port of Lorengau is very small and not likely to show any great future growth. Kieta*, the main port of Bougainville, is likely to expand very rapidly in the next few years.

Port Moresby remains the leading port of Papua and New Guinea, handling approximately 32 per cent of the country's trade at the beginning and end of the period. Rabaul's share has declined from 29 per cent in 1955–56 to 22 per cent in 1967–68, Lae's has risen from 18 to 29 per cent, and Madang's has remained constant at nine per cent.

The value of imports is more than twice that of exports. Imports are unevenly distributed between ports with 40·6 per cent passing through Port Motesby, 27·5 per cent through Lae, 16·0 per cent through Rabaul and 8·7 per cent through Madang.

Food, beverages and tobacco; manufactured goods; and machinery (including motor vehicles) are the most important groups of imports at each port. The large import of machinery including vehicles through Port Moresby relates to the large registration of motor vehicles in the district (Map 38). The large imports of food, beverages and tobacco (approximately $16·00 worth for every person in 1967–68) reflects the high dependence on imported foodstuffs by the small non-indigenous population. However, rice, canned meat and canned fish valued at $11,000,000 (37 per cent of food imports) were imported in 1967–68, and these form the staple diet of many plantation workers and urban indigenes.

* Research Fellow, New Guinea Research Unit, Australian National University, Port Moresby.

* Kieta opened as a port in November 1967. Figures before 1967–8 refer to other ports on Bougainville, mainly Buin and Buka. A new port is expected to be built north of Kieta to handle bulk shipment of copper ore and fuels, but Kieta will probably handle increasing amounts of general cargo, particularly imports.

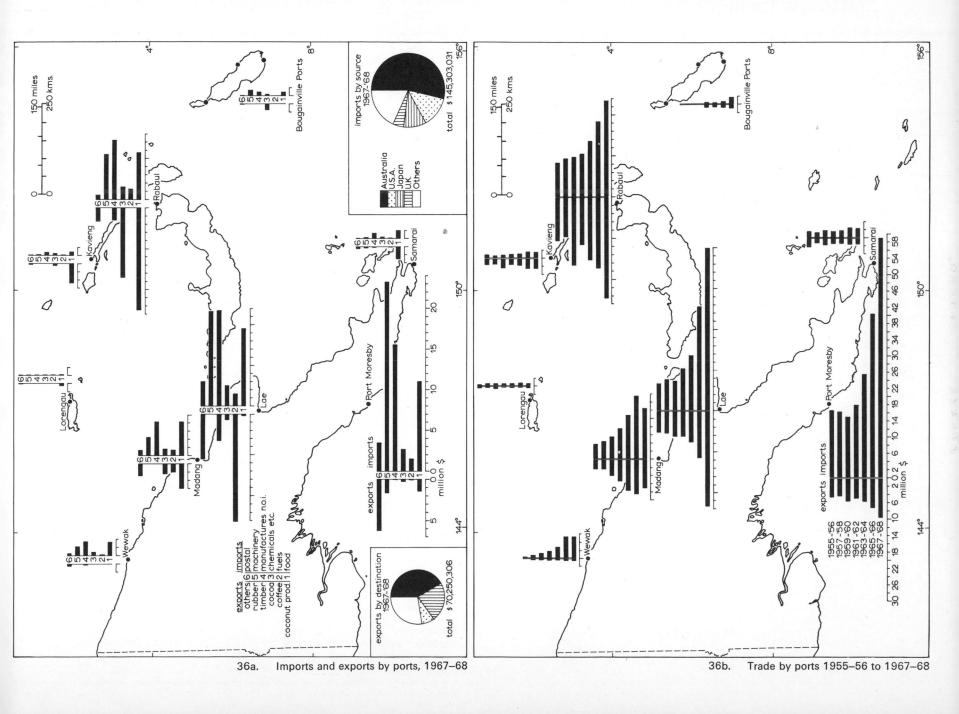

Bougainville Ports

imports by source 1967–68

total $ 145,303,031

Australia
U.S.A.
Japan
U.K.
Others

Rabaul

Kavieng

Samarai

Lorengau

6
5
4
3
2
1

Madang

Port Moresby

exports imports

exports imports
others 6 postal
rubber 5 machinery
timber 4 manufactures n.o.i.
cocoa 3 chemicals etc.
coffee 2 fuels
coconut prod. 1 food

Lae

Wewak

million $

exports by destination 1967–68

total $ 70,250,306

5

0
0

5

10

15

20

36a.   Imports and exports by ports, 1967–68

150 miles
250 kms

Bougainville Ports

Rabaul

Kavieng

Samarai

Lorengau

Madang

Port Moresby

Lae

Wewak

exports imports

1955–56
1957–58
1959–60
1961–62
1963–64
1965–66
1967–68

million $

30 26 22 18 14 10   6   2 0 2   6 10 14 18 22 26 30 34 38 42 46 50 54 58

36b.   Trade by ports 1955–56 to 1967–68

COASTAL CARGOES BETWEEN MAIN PORTS
MARION W. WARD

A sizeable carriage of cargo takes place between major ports of Papua and New Guinea but it is very hard to isolate from published statistics exactly what movements take place. The Directorate of Transport collected statistics from Customs records of all inwards and outwards cargoes between major ports for the months February–April, 1969 and these are mapped here. The total volume of cargo in the three months was 20,899 tons, which indicates a possible annual total of 83,000 tons between major ports. This is consistent with Table 1 which indicates that in 1967–68 62,100 tons weight and 69,200 tons measure of cargo was shipped internally from principal ports either within or between the two territories of Papua and New Guinea.

Table 1 *Tonnage of internal cargo handled at principal ports 1967–68*

	Discharged		Shipped		Total Handled	
	tons measure	tons weight	tons measure	tons weight	tons measure	tons weight
Inter-Territory	24·9	8·8	29·3	12·1	54·2	20·9
Intra-Territory	55·8	55·6	49·9	50·0	105·7	105·6
	80·7	63·4	69·2	62·1	159·9	126·5

Source: Bureau of Statistics, 1968, p. 27.

The flow pattern emphasizes the centrality of Lae in the transport systems of Papua and New Guinea and the importance of the movements between Lae and Port Moresby. Coastwise traffic is important between Lae and Port Moresby, Rabaul and Madang. Port Moresby also has important coastal traffic flows particularly to and from Lae, and to Rabaul and Samarai. Rabaul is the third port for coastwise cargoes. Its major suppliers of coastwise imports are Lae and Port Moresby, but Rabaul is itself the major supplier for Kieta and Kavieng. The lack of an equivalent return movement from these two ports indicates that their overseas exports are handled directly rather than trans-shipped through Rabaul. The fourth port, Madang, serves the northwest quarter of the country. Its main coastal trade is with Lae, Wewak and Vanimo. Wewak itself is also a major supplier for Vanimo. The volume of coastal cargo handled at each of the ports (and shown in Map 37) is given below.

Table 2   *Coastal cargoes, February–April, 1969*

Port	Sent	Received	Total Handled
	tons	tons	tons
Lae	7,200	3,643	10,843
Port Moresby	5,445	3,299	8,744
Rabaul	3,888	3,541	7,429
Madang	2,504	2,604	5,108
Wewak	1,029	1,933	2,962
Kieta	328	2,219	2,547
Kavieng	159	1,289	1,448
Vanimo	192	977	1,169
Samarai	84	897	981
Lorengau/Lombrom	70	453	523
Cape Hoskins	—	134	134

Source: Data from Directorate of Transport, Port Moresby.

Unfortunately no statistical information is available on the composition of this coastwise trade but much of it is general cargo and fuels. A proportion of the flow from the four major ports is redistribution of overseas imports of foodstuffs and manufactured goods. Some of Lae's exports to other major ports consist of timber and plywood. Ninety per cent of the cargo movement was carried in coastal ships; the remaining 10 per cent in overseas vessels.

Each of the major ports shown is itself the focus of yet another level of trade, carried in small boats to numerous settlements, plantations, wharves and loading points on the coasts and islands and, in the case of Wewak, along the banks of the Sepik River. The goods distributed from the main centres are a wide range of general cargo, but imports to them are often major overseas export commodities, such as copra and cocoa into Madang from Karkar Island and coastal areas, rubber and copra into Port Moresby, and copra and cocoa into Rabaul.

Bibliography:
Bureau of Statistics, 1968. *Territory of Papua and New Guinea Transport and Communications Bulletin No. 7*, Port Moresby.

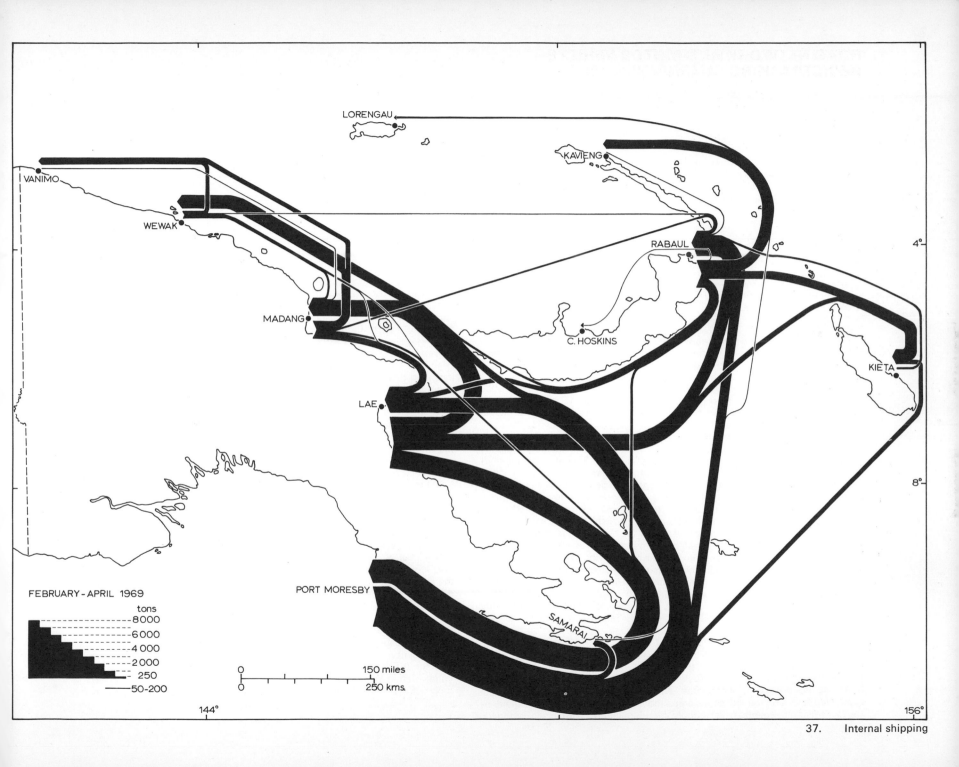

LORENGAU

KAVIENG

VANIMO

WEWAK

RABAUL

MADANG

C. HOSKINS

KIETA

LAE

PORT MORESBY

SAMARAI

FEBRUARY – APRIL 1969

tons
8000
6000
4000
2000
250
50-200

0   150 miles
0   250 kms.

144°   156°

4°

8°

37.   Internal shipping

ROAD NETWORK AND MOTOR VEHICLE
REGISTRATIONS *MARION W. WARD*

The road network of Papua and New Guinea is notably fragmented. The largest system is the Highlands Highway, which penetrates westward from Lae for some 400 miles. Other important systems centre on Port Moresby, Madang, Wewak and Popondetta. The Gazelle Peninsula has a dense network of roads, while New Ireland and Bougainville have coastal roads along the most developed sections of their coasts. It is likely that the next major road connection to be completed will link Madang with Lae and this will be followed by a second access road to the Highlands south of Madang.

Figures for traffic flow throughout the country at mid-1967 (Dept. of Public Works, 1967) show the greatest flows are in the towns, e.g. 15,800 vehicles per day between the centre of Port Moresby and its airport; 4,250 v.p.d. on the first two miles between Rabaul centre and Nonga Base Hospital; 2,700 v.p.d. on the Rabaul-Kokopo road. In Central District the Port Moresby-Brown River road carried 703 and the Sogeri road 640 v.p.d. Sections of the Highlands Highway were carrying between 500 and 600 v.p.d. Between the town of Mount Hagen and its airfield at Kagamuga there were 1,150 v.p.d. in 1967. From Wewak along the first two miles of coast road serving both a large Army base and the road to Maprik up the Sepik Valley there was a flow of 400 v.p.d. Volume of traffic is increasing and on recently opened or improved roads serving areas of great potential for economic growth, the rate is very high.

On the road between Rigo and Port Moresby for example, the annual growth rate of traffic appears to have been 85 per cent between 1964 and 1967 (Ward, 1970). It seems to have been about 30 per cent on the Highlands Highway between 1968 and 1969. Such increases generate a pressing need for improvement of road standards. Of the roads carrying high volumes of traffic mentioned above, most of those in the Gazelle Peninsula are sealed, and that between Mount Hagen and Kagamuga is about to be sealed. While the Highlands Highway is not yet sealed, work is in hand to improve its quality west of Goroka.

There are no national data on freight and passenger movements by road but certain generalizations can be made. The basic commodity movements are the feeding of exports to the ports and the distribution of imports to the hinterlands. This is most apparent in areas such as the Gazelle Peninsula, New Ireland, Bougainville, coastal Madang, the Bulolo Valley, Eastern and Western Highlands and Chimbu. In some areas, however, this pattern is overlaid by another set of movements which supply the urban centres with locally produced foodstuffs. Most inwards freight on the Port Moresby road system is for consumption in the town itself. Similar movements also take place to Rabaul, Lae, Goroka and Mount Hagen.

Surveys of freight and passenger traffic have been made recently on the Highlands Highway. It was estimated that in 1964–65 17,800 tons of freight was moved into Chimbu, Eastern and Western Highlands districts along the Highway. Outwards freight totalled 4,900 tons. A survey in October, 1968 indicated that freight was then moving in at a rate of 80,700 tons per annum, and out at 22,400 tons per annum, which suggests rates of annual increase of about 48 per cent (Directorate of Transport, 1969 : 2). A further survey in November, 1969 indicated that inwards freight (106,800 tons per annum) was up 28 per cent but outwards freight increased more slowly to 26,400 tons. It is thought this lower rate may be due to seasonal factors at the time of the survey. Inwards freight is being consigned to Highland centres, from Lae, at the following annual rates:—Kainantu, 11,300 tons; Goroka, 45,600 tons; Kundiawa, 7,000 tons; Mount Hagen, 40,900 tons; Wapenamanda and Wabag, 1,300 tons; and Southern Highlands, 700 tons (*Post-Courier,* 19 Dec., 1969). With the increase in road freight to the Highlands has come a great drop in air freight between Madang and the Highlands, stagnation of the port of Madang, and a rapid growth in trade passing through Lae (Map 36).

Motor vehicle registrations are shown for the main registration centres in Papua and New Guinea as at 31st December, 1968. The largest concentration of vehicles, 9,528, of which two-thirds are cars and station-wagons, is at Port Moresby. The other centres move down the scale, roughly to accord with the size of their urban populations. The proportion of cars and station-wagons decreases and that of trucks, utilities and tractors increases as the size of the expatriate population decreases and as remoteness and "ruralness" increase.

Bibliography:

Bureau of Statistics, 1968. *Transport and Communications Bulletin No. 7,* Port Moresby.

Department of Public Works, 1967. *Road Inventory,* Vols. 1–4, Port Moresby.

Directorate of Transport, 1969. *Information Bulletin No. 3,* Port Moresby.

Ward, Marion W., 1970. *The Rigo Road: A Study in the Economic Effects of New Road Construction,* New Guinea Research Bulletin No. 33, Canberra.

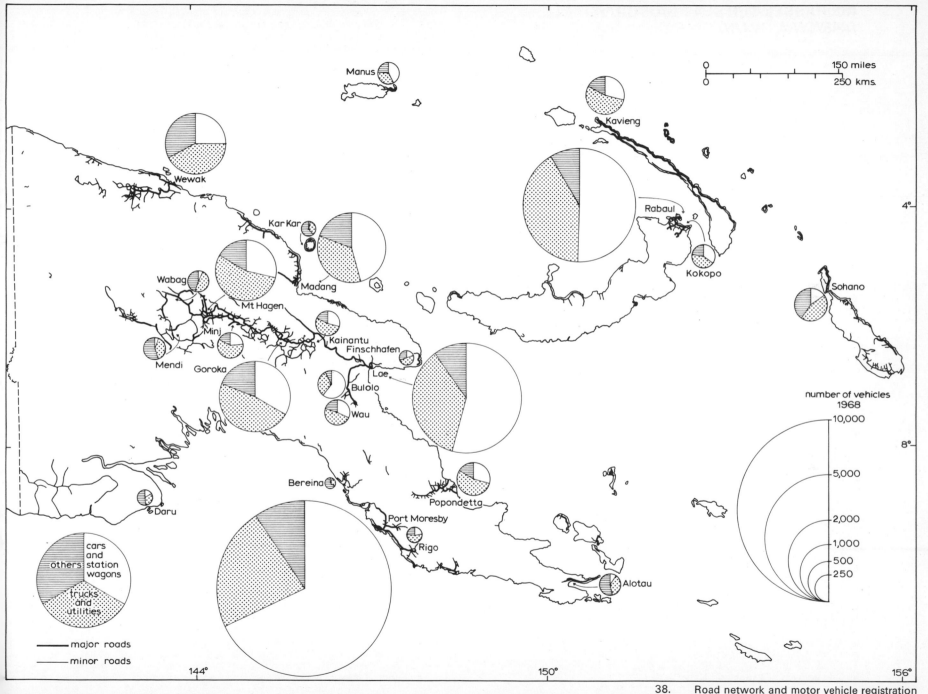

Manus

Kavieng

Wewak

Kar Kar

Rabaul

Madang

Kokopo

Sohano

Wabag

Mt Hagen

Minj

Kainantu

Finschhafen

Mendi

Goroka

Lae

Bulolo

Wau

Daru

Bereina

Popondetta

Port Moresby

Rigo

Alotau

cars
and
station
wagons

others

trucks
and
utilities

— major roads
— minor roads

number of vehicles
1968

10,000

5,000

2,000

1,000

500

250

4°

8°

144°   150°   156°

38.   Road network and motor vehicle registration

AIR PASSENGER SEAT CAPACITY
MARION W. WARD

Table 1 — Passengers, Freight and Aifcraft Movements at Selected Airports, Year ended December -3, 1968

Airport	Passengers	Freight Short Tons	Aircraft Movements (a)
Port Moresby	142,818 (1)	5,074	9,064
	85,602 (2)	1,976	1,728
	4,385 (3)	27	240
Lae	133,595 (1)	2,694	8,978
	3,820 (2)	198	157
	2,431 (3)	38	143
Rabaul	66,944 (1)	895	3,137
	639 (3)	6	43
Madang	54,047 (1)	9,628	9,616
	5 (3)	2	14
Goroka	47,199	1,262	6,201
Mt. Hagen	38,503	4,778	7,335
Wewak	26,477 (1)	962	3,761
	226 (3)	31	130

(a) A landing and take-off count as two movements.
1. Traffic on services operating wholly within Papua and New Guinea.
2. Traffic on services between Australia and Papua and New Guinea.
3. Traffic on international services.
Source : Department of Civil Aviation, 1969 : pp. 4, 22–24.

The number of aircraft seats available per week on scheduled services between centres in Papua and New Guinea is represented in Map 39. The width of line between any two places is proportional to the number of seats in both directions. Between major centres the number of seats available in each direction sometimes differs (e.g. 921 seats per week between Port Moresby and Lae ; 993 from Lae to Port Moresby) but for smaller centres they are almost invariably equal.

The importance of the link between Port Moresby and Lae is the most striking feature of the route pattern. In the development of an overall transport system the link between two major nodes tends to exceed all other links in importance, and to be followed by more than one mode of transport. In this case the transport links between Port Moresby and Lae carry the heaviest volume of both air passenger traffic, and coastal shipping (see Map 37) but as yet there is no road connection. The second striking feature is the centrality of Lae, a fact which is confirmed by network analysis of the scheduled air services route system. From Lae important routes connect with Rabaul, Goroka, and Madang, and routes of lower capacity with Bulolo, Finschhafen, Momote, Kainantu and Garaina. The third feature is the number of low-level connections in such regions as south-east Papua, Southern and Western Highlands, and the Sepik.

The flow pattern shown on this map is supported by the following data for leading airfields in Papua and New Guinea.

Port Moresby and Lae each handled more than twice as many passengers than any other airport, although Madang was handling a larger volume of freight and more aircraft movements in 1968 due to its role as a supply centre for the Highlands. Before the road link to the Highlands was open Madang's importance in this respect was considerably greater than it is now.

One of the main factors contributing to the heavy use of the Port Moresby–Lae link is Port Moresby's role as main terminal for flights to and from Australia (Table 1). There are two Boeing 727 return flights from Australia on most days, and this number is likely to be increased in 1970. In addition, a twice-weekly Boeing 707 service links Port Moresby with Sydney, Manila and Hong Kong. The connection with the Australia flights in Port Moresby is the governing factor for all internal routes and schedules, and was used as the basis for the recent recommendation by the U.N.D.P. Transport Survey (1969, pp. 2.13–2.14) that there should be one national internal air line (instead of the existing extension of the unique Australian two-airline policy).

The types of aircraft in use in the scheduled services shown on this map range from Fokker Friendships (36 seats) and DC3s (32 seats) on the major links (all airports named in Table 1, plus Momote and Kavieng), through Twin Otters (15 seats), Piaggios (9), SC7s (18) to a range of small single or twin-engined aircraft seating from five to eight passengers. In addition to the scheduled services, charter flights serve many more airfields than are shown on this map. In general the volume of passengers and freight carried in this way is not large compared with the scheduled services, but the flexibility of light aircraft movements is of considerable importance in reducing isolation and inaccessibility within Papua and New Guinea.

Bibliography:

Dept. of Civil Aviation, 1969. *Statistics of Australian Regular Air Transport Services, Year Ended – .3 December, 1968 (C.A.559)*, Canberra.
United Nations Development Program, International Bank for Reconstruction and Development, 1969. *Transport Survey of the Territories of Papua and New Guinea, Summary of Conclusions and Recommendations'*

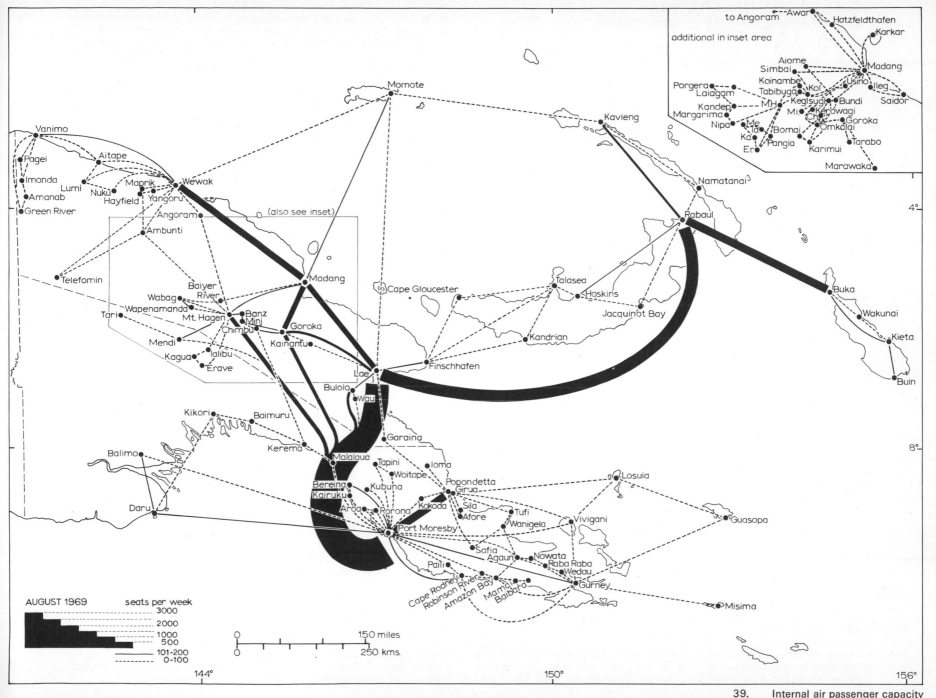

Momote

Vanimo
Pagei
Imonda
Amanab
Green River
Aitape
Lumi
Nuku
Hayfield
Maprik
Yangoru
Wewak
Angoram
Ambunti
Telefomin
Baiyer River
Wabag
Wapenamanda
Tari
Mt. Hagen
Banz
Minj
Chimbu
Mendi
Kagua
Ialibu
Erave
Kainantu
Goroka
Madang

(also see inset)

Cape Gloucester

Lae
Bulolo
Wau

Kikori
Baimuru
Kerema
Garaina

Balimo
Malalaua
Tapini
Ioma
Woitape
Popondetta
Bereina
Kubuna
Girua
Kairuku
Kokoda
Sila
Daru
Aroa
Rorona
Afore
Tufi
Wanigela
Port Moresby
Safia
Agaun
Nowata
Raba Raba
Wedau
Paili
Cape Rodney
Robinson River
Mama
Balbara
Amazon Bay
Gurney

Finschhafen
Talasea
Hoskins
Jacquinot Bay
Kandrian

Kavieng

Namatanai
Rabaul
Buka
Wakunai
Kieta
Buin

Losuia
Vivigani
Guasopa
Misima

Inset (upper right)

to Angoram ← Awar
additional in inset area
Hatzfeldthafen
Karkar
Aiome
Simbai
Porgera
Koinambe
Kol
Usino
Ileg
Laiagam
Tabibuga
Madang
Saidor
Kandep
MH
Mi.
Kerowagi
Margarima
Ch.
Goroka
Nipa
Me.
Omkalai
Ja.
Bomai
Ka.
Er.
Pangia
Karimui
Tarabo
Marawaka

AUGUST 1969   seats per week

3000
2000
1000
500
101-200
0-100

150 miles
250 kms.

144°   150°   156°
4°
8°

39.   Internal air passenger capacity

ELECTRICITY GENERATION *PAPUA AND NEW GUINEA ELECTRICITY COMMISSION*

Moresby's first hydro station on the Laloki River, Rouna No. 1, was opened and the Electrical Undertakings Branch began to function. This branch maintained services and drew up plans for the Laloki Hydro-Electric Scheme and in 1963 the Sirinumu Dam was opened on the Laloki River about 30 miles from Port Moresby. The purpose of this dam of rock-fill construction was to maintain and adequate and steady flow of water during both the wet and dry seasons. In the same year the Papua and New Guinea Electricity Commission was formed to control and develop the supply of electricity in the Territory. By agreement with the Administration, the Commission took over complete control of all generation plant in Port Moresby, Lae, Rabaul, Kokopo, Madang, Wewak, Goroka, Kavieng and Samarai. The Commission also agreed to maintain and operate small centres on behalf of the Administration. In June, 1969 there were 127 such centres.

The principal Administration centres are all diesel, with Mount Hagen having an installed capacity of 0·675 MW, Popondetta, Daru and Keravat each with a capacity of 0·45 MW, and Kieta, Lorengau, Alotau, Kainantu and Kundiawa all having diesel stations with capacities between 0·2 and 0·3 MW. There are also small hydro stations owned by the Administration in Mount Hagen (0·18 MW), Mendi (0·16 MW), Tapini and Aiyura. The Commission operates three hydro-electric power stations, two in Port Moresby and a small one in Goroka with a capacity of 0·4 MW supplementing diesel generation. The largest station in the Territory is the underground Rouna No. 2 completed in June, 1969 with a capacity of 30 MW, which together with Rouna No. 1 (5·5 MW) provides Port Moresby's present power requirements. The other towns with Commission centres are supplied with diesel-generated power with a total installed capacity of 13·8 MW. Rabaul has the largest installed diesel capacity of 4·2 MW, Lae has a capacity of 2·7 MW, Madang 2·28 MW, Wewak 2·3 MW, Goroka 1·4 MW and Samarai plus Kavieng both less than 0·5 MW. Kokopo diesel station closed down in May, 1969 and it was connected by a 22 kV transmission line from Rabaul. During 1968–69 the Commission generated 108·5 million kWh and purchased 22·7 million kWh from Placer Development at Baiune for reticulation in Lae.

Since the formation of the Electricity Commission the demand for electricity has increased at a rate of over 19 per cent each year. To keep up with these increasing demands additional plant has been or shortly will be installed in all major centres. To allow the full potential of Rouna No. 2 to be realized the Sirinumu Dam is being raised from 76 feet to 106 feet and this work should be completed by December, 1970. This should meet the power demands of Port Moresby and its surrounding areas until at least 1973. It is possible that another station of 10–18 MW could be installed downstream from Rouna No. 1.

The most promising area for large-scale hydro-electricity production is the Upper Ramu, about 20 miles ENE of Kainantu. Here the Ramu River falls approximately 2,500 feet in a distance of about five miles. The Scheme, which would serve the area between Lae, Madang and Mount Hagen, has a power potential of some 250 MW at 55 per cent annual load factor. Investigations of the site are almost complete, but finance for the project still has to be obtained. Officials from the International Bank for Reconstruction and Development have visited the area that the scheme will serve. If a firm decision to finance the scheme is given during 1969–70, construction of the project could begin in 1971. Preliminary investigations for potential hydro-electric power sites are taking place on the Vanapa and Angabunga rivers in the Central District, the Musa River in the Northern District and Kapuira River and Lake Hargy in New Britain.

Note: A pamphlet containing detailed descriptions of Laloki and Upper Ramu schemes can be obtained from the Electricity Commission. It is entitled *History of the Papua and New Guinea Electricity Commission.*

The first large-scale electric power production in Papua and New Guinea was in the early 1930s when gold-dredging companies in the Bulolo area harnessed the Baiune River. Elsewhere only the main centres had any electricity. During the Second World War almost all electricity generating plant was destroyed or severely damaged. After the war a new start had to be made but power production was essentially a make-shift affair until 1957 when Port

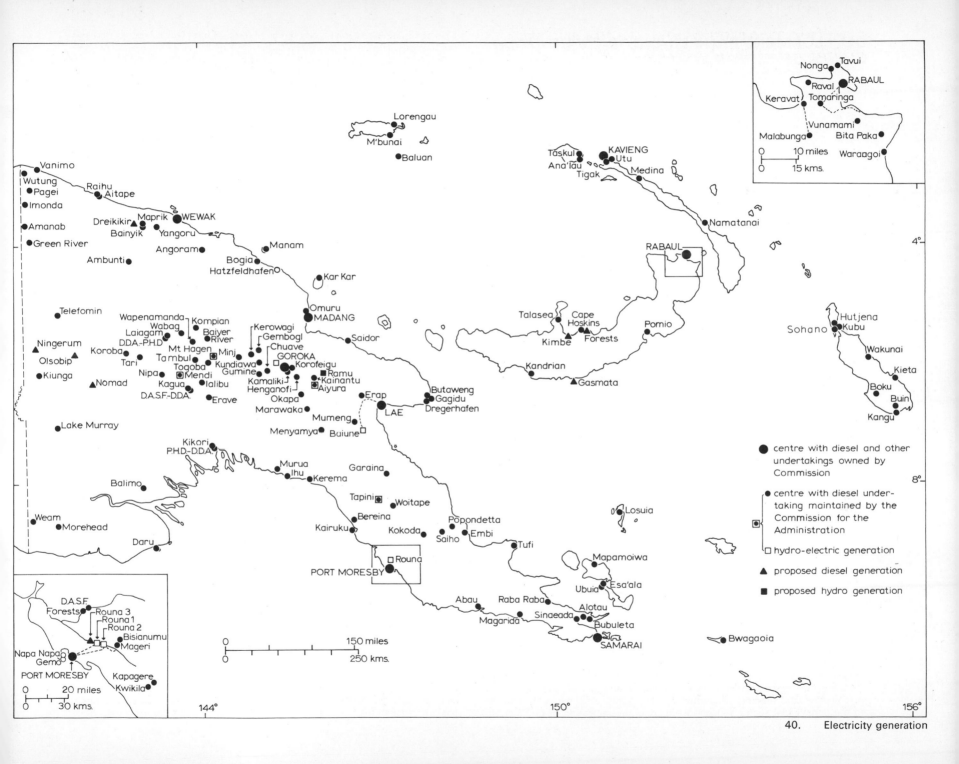

Lorengau
M'bunai
Baluan

Vanimo
Wutung
Pagei
Imonda
Amanab
Green River
Raihu
Aitape
Dreikikir
Maprik
WEWAK
Bainyik
Yangoru
Angoram
Manam
Bogia
Hatzfeldhafen
Kar Kar
Ambunti

Telefomin
Wapenamanda
Kompian
Omuru
MADANG
Wabag
Kerowagi
Gembogl
Laiagam
Baiyer River
Chuave
Saidor
DDA.-P.H.D
Mt Hagen
GOROKA
Ningerum
Koroba
Minj
Korofeigu
Olsobip
Tambul
Kundiawa
Ramu
Tari
Togoba
Gumine
Kainantu
Kiunga
Nipa
Mendi
Kamaliki
Aiyura
Nomad
Kagua
Ialibu
Henganofi
Erap
Butaweng
Gagidu
D.A.S.F.-D.D.A.
Erave
Okapa
LAE
Dregerhafen
Marawaka
Mumeng
Lake Murray
Menyamya
Buiune

Talasea
Cape Hoskins
Pomio
Kimbe
Forests
Kandrian
Gasmata

RABAUL

Taskul
KAVIENG
Ana'Iau
Utu
Tigak
Medina
Namatanai

Sohano
Hutjena
Kubu
Wakunai
Kieta
Boku
Buin
Kangu

Kikori
P.H.D.-D.D.A.
Murua
Ihu
Garaina
Kerema
Tapini
Woitape
Balimo
Bereina
Popondetta
Kairuku
Kokoda
Saiho
Embi
Tufi
Weam
Morehead
Daru
Losuia
Mapamoiwa
Rouna
PORT MORESBY
Ubuia
Esa'ala
Abau
Raba Raba
Alotau
Magarida
Sinaeada
Bubuleta
SAMARAI
Bwagaoia

RABAUL
Nonga
Tavui
Raval
Keravat
Tomaringa
Vunamami
Malabunga
Bita Paka
Waraagoi
0   10 miles
0   15 kms.

D.A.S.F
Forests
Rouna 3
Rouna 1
Rouna 2
Bisianumu
Napa Napa
Mageri
Gemo
PORT MORESBY
Kapagere
Kwikila
0   20 miles
0   30 kms.

- centre with diesel and other undertakings owned by Commission
- centre with diesel under-taking maintained by the Commission for the Administration
□ hydro-electric generation
▲ proposed diesel generation
■ proposed hydro generation

0   150 miles
0   250 kms.

144°   150°   156°
4°
8°

40.   Electricity generation

DEVELOPMENT BANK LOANS *PAPUA AND NEW GUINEA DEVELOPMENT BANK*

The Papua and New Guinea Development Bank was established in July, 1967 and its main function is to provide finance for primary production and for the establishment or development of industrial and commercial undertakings, particularly small undertakings. Under its charter, the Bank's policy is to be directed towards the greatest advantage of the people, the stability and balanced development of the Territory's economy and the advancement of the indigenous population. In fulfilling its function, the Bank only provides finance that would "not otherwise be available on reasonable and suitable terms and conditions" and is primarily concerned with the prospects of an enterprise becoming, or continuing to be successful and does not necessarily have regard to the value of the security available.

The Bank operates through its Head Office in Port Moresby and Regional Offices at Lae, Rabaul and Mount Hagen. In addition, the Bank has the agency services of all Trading Bank branches, Officers of the Department of Agriculture, Stock and Fisheries, Department of Trade and Industry and the Division of District Administration.

At the end of September, 1967, 27 months after it commenced operation, the Bank has approved 1,374 loans totalling over $8·5 million and held equity over $1·6 million in eight locally incorporated companies.

The maps illustrate the amount and number of loans to each District by industry and ethnic group. They show clearly the concentration of loans in districts with major urban centres, such as Central District (Port Moresby), Morobe (Lae), East New Britain (Rabaul) and the Eastern and Western Highlands (Goroka and Mount Hagen). The exception is West New Britain where 545 loans totalling a little over $1 million have been approved to indigenous smallholders, growing oil palm on a land settlement scheme; this explains the very large circle in the West New Britain area.

Whilst agriculture continues to be the mainstay of the Territory economy (this will change dramatically over the next few years because of mineral discoveries), the greatest proportion of loan approvals have been allocated to the commercial sector, reflecting a gradual diversification of the economy and, in particular, the growth of the transport and tourist industries. Commercial loans accounted for nearly 46 per cent (almost $4·0 million) of total approvals, followed by rural approvals of $3·4 million (about 40 per cent of total) and industrial $1·3 million (14 per cent). On the rural side, the cattle, oil palm and tea industries obtained the most financial assistance while timber predominated in the industrial classification.

The classification of loan approvals according to the race of the borrower shows that by far the greatest numbers of loans (about 77 per cent) have been granted to Papuans and New Guineans. However, by amount, non-indigenous borrowing far exceeds that of other classifications. Whilst this is only to be expected at this stage of the Territory's development, the Bank is constantly endeavouring to increase both the number and amounts of loans to Papuans and New Guineans, the progress has been most encouraging.

One of the most challenging and complex problems facing the Bank relates to customary (or clan) land. It is, therefore, frequently impossible to gain any normal banking security over land which is usually considered essential for the provision of long-term rural credit. The problem is characterized by the lack of any legal guarantee that a borrower will retain his land usage rights, after he commences a development project. However, this uncertainty does not deter the Bank from providing finance for development on clan land for periods of up to 10 years, if there is sufficient evidence to show that the borrower has usage rights under local custom. To facilitate this policy, the Bank has formulated a Land Usage Agreement, upon which clan leaders acknowledge the borrower's rights to use the land.

To support the loan a guarantee is needed from at least two responsible people who would, in the event of death, default or incapacitation of the borrower, be prepared to take over the responsibility of continuing with the original farm development plan and meeting loan repayments as they fall due. It is preferred that one of these guarantors should be the person who is the natural heir to the land in question. While it is doubtful that the clan land usage agreement has any legal status, so far the system has worked to the Bank's satisfaction.

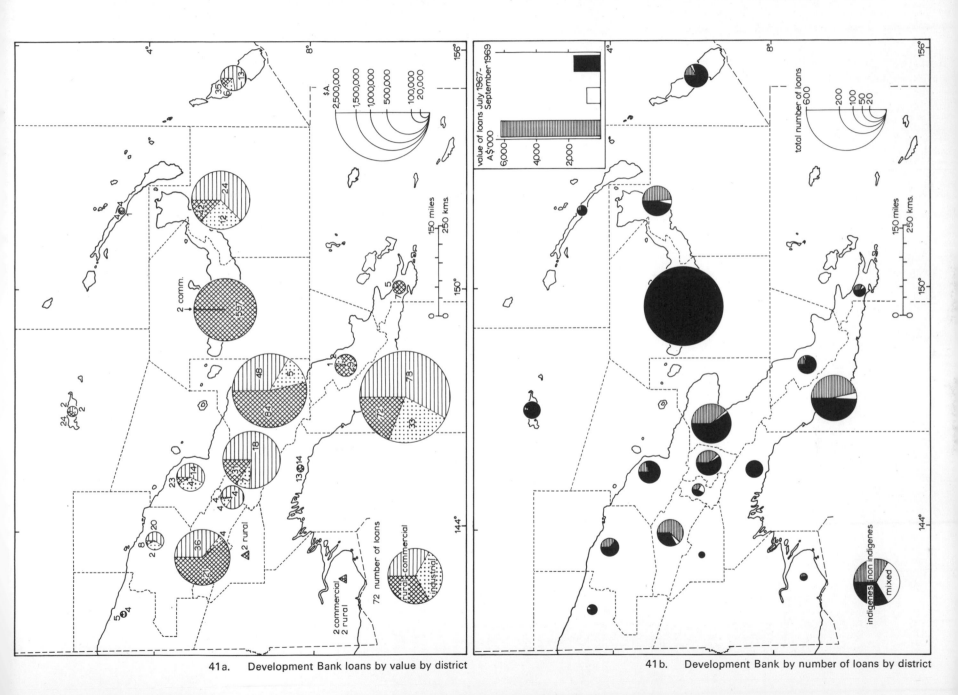

41a.   Development Bank loans by value by district

41b.   Development Bank by number of loans by district

INTRODUCTION TO SERVICES *R. GERARD WARD and D. A. M. LEA*

Basic to the further development of any country is the provision of the infrastructure of administration and services. In parts of Papua and New Guinea virtually none of the paraphernalia of a modern state existed 20 years ago. Maps 2 a–d show how the framework of district administration by the central government has been modified to suit changing conditions in the years since 1946. In the last decade, one of the most striking features of administration activity has been the development of local government based on elected councils. Today, most of the population live within the territory of a local government council (*cf.* Maps 5 and 42). At the national level the process of political change is represented by the establishment of the House of Assembly with predominantly elected (and indigenous) membership (Map 45).

In part these, like other developments, have only been possible because of a rapid expansion of education. Before 1946 this field of activity was left almost entirely to the missions, and even today many areas have far more mission than government schools (Map 43). Spectacular though the growth of school rolls has been, there are still striking inequalities in the proportion of school-age children actually at school in different districts (Map 44a). Similarly, education is still dominantly for males. In some districts less than a quarter of the school-children are females (Map 44b). These differences are inevitable at this stage of the country's development as it is impossible to provide services everywhere to the same level at the same time. To attempt to do so would be a very uneconomic policy.

Wider political groupings and the new jobs which the young educated adults desire can only be provided by an increasingly commercialized economy. This also requires new forms of organization and one such is the co-operative movement (Map 46). Again, as in the case of indigenous-owned trade stores (Map 46) the level of development varies markedly from district to district. As with other aspects of socio-economic development, those districts which have had long contact and considerable non-indigenous investment are also those with the greatest development of indigenous trade stores and co-operatives. Some exceptions to this generalization are apparent, however, and would provide interesting areas for further research into the processes of and constraints on socio-economic development.

As noted on page 1, our knowledge of Papua and New Guinea is still far from comprehensive and this is indicated for three fields in Maps 49 to 51. Basic topographical information with maps at a reasonable scale is still lacking for considerable areas but the use of aerial photography is gradually reducing the unknown (Map 51). At present, the study of the pre-history of Papua and New Guinea is still in its infancy (Map 50) but in terms of what Papua and New Guinea offer to the outside world, one of its most important contributions may ultimately be the understanding of human societies which should come from the work of the numerous anthropologists and sociologists (Map 49) who have studied in this country.

LOCAL GOVERNMENT COUNCILS *JOHN RUMENS* *

The first Local Government Council in Papua and New Guinea, the Hanuabada Native Village Council, representing 3,500 people, was established in 1950. By December, 1969 there were 144 councils representing 1,998,000 people, or 86·5 per cent of the estimated total population. At that date 52 were administering a population of 525,000 in Papua, whilst in New Guinea 92 councils were responsible for 1,473,000 people. The scope for additional councils is limited as the remaining non-council areas are sparsely populated. Under the *Native Local Government Councils Ordinance,* 1949–60, councils were restricted to the indigenous population. *The Local Government Ordinance,* 1963, which became operative in January, 1965, replaced the previous legislation and made possible the introduction of multi-racial councils. The local government system is still essentially rural, although it is proposed that councils will be established in the major urban centres in 1970.

There is great variation in population between councils—the extremes being Murua (No. 8 in Milne Bay District), with a population of 2,506 and the Gazelle Peninsula Council (No. 2 in East New Britain), which serves 68,798 people. Generally the contrast in size is between the highlands and coastal councils. In the Highlands the average council population rises from 15,000 in Southern Highlands to 27,000 in Eastern Highlands; whereas, with the exception of the densely populated East Sepik and East New BritainD istricts, and the anomalous Manus District with its single council, the average population per council in coastal districts does not reach 15,000.

From the start, even when the *Native Village Councils Ordinance* was the controlling legislation, an area rather than a single village type of organization was adopted. This was essential if councils were to raise the finance necessary to carry out functions permitted under the legislation.

There are difficulties in obtaining the support of the people, because the idea of working in large groups which are not ethnically or linguistically based is alien. However, a council's efficiency depends on factors, such as communication links and adequate revenue for undertaking capital works and providing services, which require different, or larger, groups. Difficulties stem not only from the traditional absence of co-operation but also from the single village system of administration used by the central authority in pre-council times.

Nevertheless, to quote the first Commissioner for Local Government ". . . most councils at the time of their establishment have covered at least two separate linguistic and social groups, often three and sometimes more. Even so, the resulting Council area might only include a population of 5,000 to 6,000" (Plant, 1965). Councils of this size have a low revenue potential. As the financial limitations of small councils were recognized, amalgamations occurred leading to the development of larger local government units; for example, the present Gazelle Peninsula Local Government Council resulted from the amalgamation of five councils.

For the year ended June 30, 1968, total council revenue was $2,934,000 (New Guinea $2,249,000; Papua $685,000). The main sources of funds were as follows:

Taxes	$1,673,000
Administration Grants and Subsidies	$447,000
Goods and Services	$217,000
Property Income	$49,000
Bank Loans	$91,000
Surplus from previous year	$245,000

The main activities on which funds were spent included:

Transport and communications	$939,000
Education, Welfare, Health	$536,000
Forestry, Agriculture, Water Supply	$198,000

Bibliography:

Plant, H. T., 1965. *Problems in Rural Councils.* Mimeo. Port Moresby.

* Lecturer, Administrative College, Port Moresby.

KEY TO MAP

Western District
1. Gogodala (M*)
2. Kiunga (M)
3. Kiwai (M*)
4. Lake Murray (M)
5. Morehead
6. Oriomo-Bituri (M*)

Gulf District
1. Baimuru (M)
2. East Kerema
3. Kaipi
4. Kerema Bay (M*)
5. Kikori (M)
6. Korimiri
7. Orokolo

Central District
1. Amazon Bay (M*)
2. Kairuku
3. Marshall Lagoon (M*)
4. Mekeo
5. Port Moresby
6. Rigo
7. Tapini (M*)
8. Woitape (M)

Milne Bay
1. Bwana Bwana
2. Daga (M)
3. Dobu
4. Duau (M*)
5. Goodenough Island (M*)
6. Kiriwina
7. Louisiade (M*)
8. Makamaka (M*)
9. Maramatana
10. Milne Bay (M*)
11. Murua
12. Suau
13. Weraura (M*)
14. West Fergusson (M)

Northern District
1. Afore (M)
2. Cape Nelson (M*)
3. Higaturu (M*)
4. Ilimo (M*)
5. Oro Bay (M*)
6. Tamata (M)

Southern Highlands District
1. Erave (M)
2. Ialibu (M*)
3. Kagua (M*)
4. Komo (M*)
5. Koroba (M*)
6. Lake Kutubu (M)
7. Margarima (M)
8. Mendi (M*)
9. Nipa (M)
10. Pangia (M)
11. Tari (M*)

Eastern Highlands District
1. Asaro Watabung (M)
2. Erandora (M)
3. Goroka (M*)
4. Henganofi (M*)
5. Kainantu (M)
6. Lamari (M)
7. Lufa (M*)
8. Okapa (M)

Chimbu District
1. Elimbari (M*)
2. Gumine (M)
3. Kerowagi (M*)
4. Kundiawa (M)
5. Mt. Wilhelm (M)
6. Sinasina (M)

Western Highlands District
1. Baiyer River (M)
2. Dei (M*)
3. Jimi
4. Kandep (M)
5. Kompiam (M)
6. Lagaip
7. Mt. Giluwe
8. Mt. Hagen (M*)
9. Mul
10. Wabag (M*)
11. Wahgi (M*)
12. Wapenamanda (M*)

West Sepik District
1. Amanab
2. Green River
3. Nuku (M)
4. Pagei
5. Siau (M*)
6. Telefomin (M)
7. Vanimo (M*)
8. Walsa
9. Wapei (M*)

East Sepik District
1. Ambunti (M)
2. Angoram (M)
3. Dreikikir (M)
4. Gaui (M*)
5. Greater Maprik (M*)
6. Keram (M)
7. Saussia (M*)
8. Wewak-But (M*)
9. Wosera (M*)
10. Yangoru (M*)

Madang District
1. Almami (M)
2. Ambenob
3. Astrolabe Bay (M)
4. Bundi (M)
5. Iabu (M*)
6. Karkar (M*)
7. Rai Coast (M*)
8. Arabaka (M*)
9. Sumgilbar (M*)
10. Usino (M)
11. Yawar (M4)

Morobe District
1. Finschhafen (M*)
2. Huon (M*)
3. Kabwum (M)
4. Markham (M*)
5. Morobe (M*)
6. Mumeng
7. Nawae
8. Pindiu (M*)
9. Siassi
10. Tewae (M)
11. Wantoat
12. Waria (M)
13. Watut (M)

West New Britain District
1. Bali-Witu (M)
2. Gloucester (M)
3. Hoskins (M)
4. Kandrian (M)
5. Nakanai (M)
6. Talasea (M*)

East New Britain District
1. Bainings (M*)
2. Gazelle Peninsula (M*)
3. Mengen (M)

New Ireland District
1. Central New Ireland (M*)
2. Lavongai
3. Mussau-Emira (M)
4. Namatanai (M*)
5. Tikana (M*)

Bougainville District
1. Bana (M)
2. Buin
3. Buka (M*)
4. Kieta (M*)
5. Siwai (M*)
6. Teop-Tinputz (M*)
7. Wakunai (M*)

Manus District
1. Manus (M*)

M* Amended to Multi-racial
M Established as Multi-racial

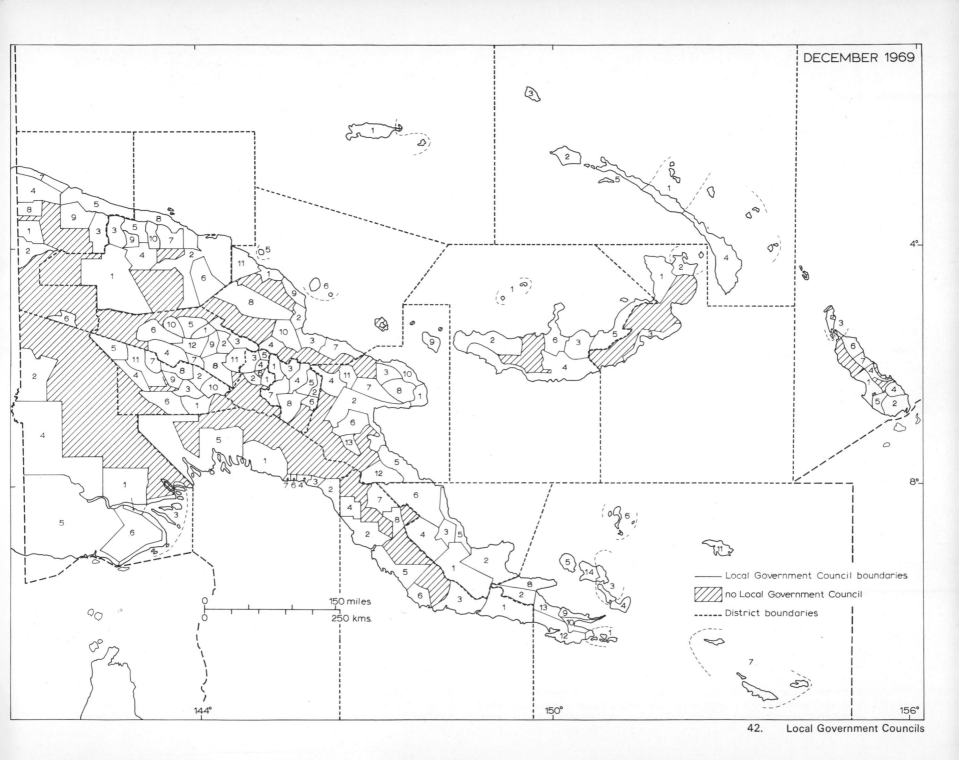

DECEMBER 1969

Local Government Council boundaries
no Local Government Council
District boundaries

150 miles
250 kms.

42.   Local Government Councils

SCHOOLS *JOHN RUMENS*

primary education was not abandoned, emphasis changed and post-primary education burgeoned. A rise in expenditure on education from $3,092,000 in 1960 to $4,080,000 in 1961 was tangible evidence of increasing interest in education, and the 1969 Budget allocation of $16,541,000 indicates that this has been maintained. Education became the Administration's largest item of expenditure in 1964, and the 1969 allocation was some 33 per cent higher than that received by Public Health, the next largest department in terms of expenditure. However, in 1969, even though the Administration's financial contribution had become major, the missions were teaching 55 per cent of the children enrolled in Territory schools.

Structure of Education

The present educational structure has developed rapidly and still has to expand to the point where it provides for the majority of school age children. This structure, in which expatriates occupy the senior positions, is managed by the Administration and a large number of mission authorities. While this may give the impression of a fragmented system there is fairly effective central control. The missions, in order to receive financial aid, have to follow a common syllabus and comply with departmental requirements concerning facilities and teacher certification. A further degree of control and co-ordination exists in that the Administration does not provide, or subsidise, further facilities in areas which it considers are already adequately serviced.

The last session of the House of Assembly in 1969 received the report of an expert committee set up to advise on the development of a national education system. Broadly it has recommended an integrated system in which all teachers' (administration and mission) salaries will become administration responsibility, and provision of most primary school buildings and teachers' houses a task for local government councils. Currently most mission teachers receive much less than their administration counterparts and have voiced considerable dissatisfaction with this situation; therefore, adoption of the salary recommendation mentioned above will enable missions to continue to make a substantial contribution to education.

Primary Education

Primary schools are of two types. Those teaching the Territory syllabus catered for 206,786 indigenous children in 1969 and those which teach the N.S.W. syllabus had 6,608 pupils, 91 per cent of whom were non-indigenous. In government schools, and mission schools which receive a grant in aid, all instruction is in English—a foreign language to practically all pupils and the majority of their teachers. At present the primary phase involves seven years, however this is to be reduced to six years by 1973. The demand for primary education is considerable, for at present only about 40 per cent of the estimated primary school age children, six to twelve years, are attending school. This percentage masks great differences between districts which are clearly shown on Map 44a.

Missions were clearly dominant in the provision of education in all but two districts (Central and Eastern Highlands) in 1966. In coastal areas the long period of operation by missions helps explain their dominant position. However, in the highlands, where administration and mission development were concurrent, the missions have been surprisingly active in the provision of educational facilities. Map 44b clearly shows that missions are educating more girls than the Administration; and also that in all districts girls constitute less than 50 per cent of the school enrolments—although it is very close to 50 per cent in the New Guinea Islands. In the highlands, by contrast, only 25–30 per cent of school attenders are girls, and these are a mere 10–15 per cent of the estimated school age girls in the population.

At present, with the educational system expanding, there are many more children in the lower than in the upper primary classes—in 1969 Standard I

Before World War II limited funds restricted government educational activity in New Guinea to a few schools around Rabaul, and to subsidies for missions in Papua. Thus for all practical purposes the government did not enter the field of education until after World War II. In 1951 the Education Department, with 4,562 pupils, was allocated $786,000, which, in terms of expenditure, made it the third most important department after Public Health and District Administration. By 1958 departmental enrolments had risen to 17,796 and expenditure to $2,032,000—making it the second largest spending department in the administration after Public Health. The overall policy of gradualism espoused in the 1950s was reflected in relatively slow expansion aimed at ultimately providing universal primary education.

Growing official awareness that political and economic development required educated leaders and a trained work-force resulted in a dramatic expansion in expenditure on education in the 1960s; and, although the aim of universal

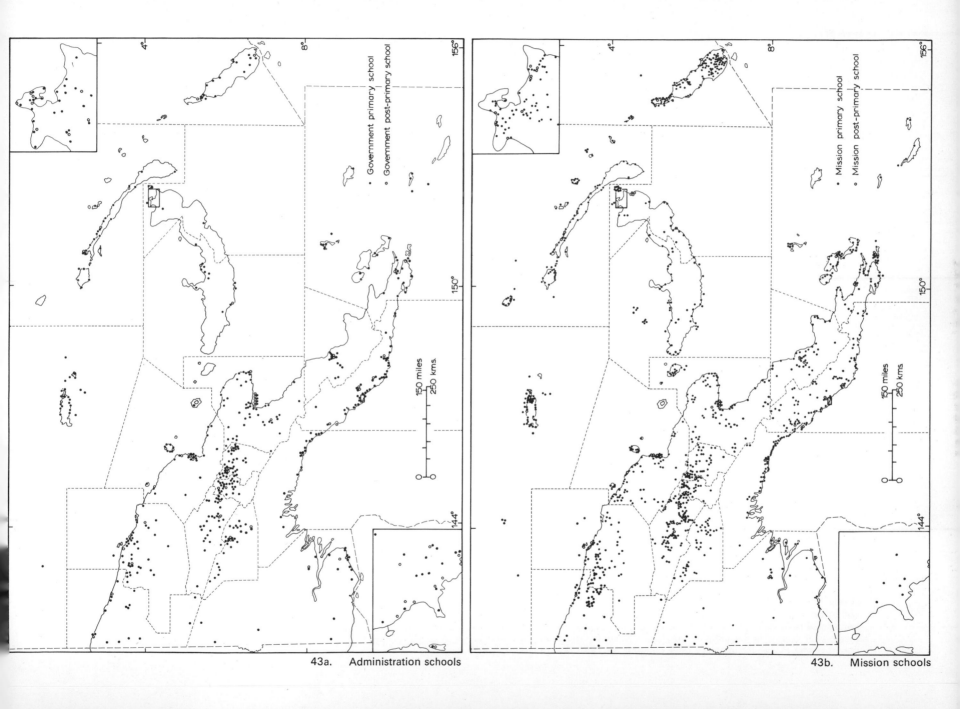

Government primary school

Government post-primary school

150 miles
250 kms.

43a.   Administration schools

Mission primary school

Mission post-primary school

150 miles
250 kms.

43b.   Mission schools

enrolments were 43,574 while there were only 16,975 in Standard VI. This tapering effect is further accentuated by the shortage of teachers for upper classes and the fact that education is not compulsory. As a result some children are not completing a full primary course.

High Schools

There is a dual high school system: Territory high schools, of which there were 58 in 1969 with 15,437 students; and multi-racial high schools, located in Port Moresby, Lae and Rabaul, with an enrolment of 832 in 1969.* In 1963 Sogeri High School produced the first matriculation class taught in a Territory high school, presenting 14 candidates for the N.S.W. Leaving Certificate.

The first external examinations for high schools set within the Territory were for the Intermediate Certificate in 1963. The School Certificate examination was first set by Territory authorities in 1965 and, as a result of the implementation of the recommendations of the Commission on Higher Education in Papua and New Guinea, became the effective terminal course in Territory high schools. From the time the N.S.W. system was adopted attempts to develop a Territory curriculum began, and by 1969 many subjects bore little resemblance to the N.S.W. progenitors.

A reorganization of secondary education occurred in 1969. The four-year high school course was divided into two discrete, two-year cycles and a senior high school with forms V and VI introduced. It is planned that all students who enter high school will be guaranteed two years of education, after which 50 per cent will continue into the second high school cycle, 25 per cent will move into technical schools and the remaining 25 per cent will leave school. At the end of the second high school cycle approximately 10 per cent of students in Form IV will continue to Forms V and VI in senior high schools. The advent of senior high schools will ultimately relieve the tertiary institutions (University, Institute of Technology, Medical College and Dental College) of the task of providing a preliminary year for their students.

In 1969, 6,080 (or 41 per cent) of the 14,710 pupils in Standard VI in 1968 were admitted to high schools. Current planning indicates that only 25 per cent of the expanding Standard VI population will be admitted to high schools from 1975 onwards. In 1974 it is estimated that there will be 33,500 pupils in Standard VI; of these approximately 8,500 will be admitted to high schools in 1975. Two factors help explain this relatively slow rate of expansion. Firstly, most high schools are boarding institutions and, therefore, extremely costly to build and operate. Secondly, high schools, which are almost entirely staffed by expatriates recruited from Australia where there is a critical shortage, are not likely to receive a significant number of New Guinean teachers in the next six years.

The unbalanced sex ratio noted in primary schools is even more pronounced in high schools: in 1969 only 26 per cent of high schools tudents were female—the range being from 5 per cent in Chimbu to 47 per cent in Manus. Similarly the tapering is more dramatic: in 1969 Form I enrolments were 6,011 compared with 1,324 in Form IV. However, other factors, in addition to limited facilities, help explain this situation. For example the Intermediate Certificate, which is the prescribed qualification for many occupations, is obtained at the end of Form III and current demand for individuals with this qualification is high.

Technical and Vocational Schools

There were nine technical schools in the Territory in 1969 catering for 1,437 pupils. From 1970 only pupils who have completed Form II at high school will be enrolled for trade training.

For a small proportion of those Standard VI pupils not admitted to high schools a two-year course is available at Vocational schools. These are designed to impart useful skills—for example boat building. In 1969 569 girls and 2,302 boys were in 60 vocational schools.

Teacher Training

The Administration, with three, and the missions, with twelve, teachers' colleges offer A, B and C certificate courses. Intending teachers who have completed Standard VI primary or Form I high school undertake the one-year A certificate course which qualifies them to teach up to Standard II. To undertake the B certificate course of two years students must have completed Form II at high school, whilst the B and C courses are qualified to teach any primary class—and some better qualified C course teachers have been placed in high schools. To date there have been few graduates of the C course; whereas the A certificate is held by more than 2,000 teachers. Even though the Administration colleges no longer offer the A course, primary schools will for many years rely on these minimally qualified teachers. The likelihood of this dependence is highlighted by the fact that in 1969 teacher training institutions only had 1,694 students, an increase of only 800, on their 1960 enrolments. Herein lie two of the major problems confronting education—how to obtain a quantitively and qualitatively adequate teaching service.

Bibliography:

Education Dept., T. P. & N. G., 1969. *The Committee of Inquiry on Education* (Weeden Report).

Education in Papua–New Guinea, 1969. *Current Affairs Bulletin,* Vol. 43, No. 6.

Education in Papua and New Guinea, 1968. *The Australian Journ. Education* (Special Issue), Vol. 12, No. 1.

* These latter follow the N.S.W. six-year secondary course.

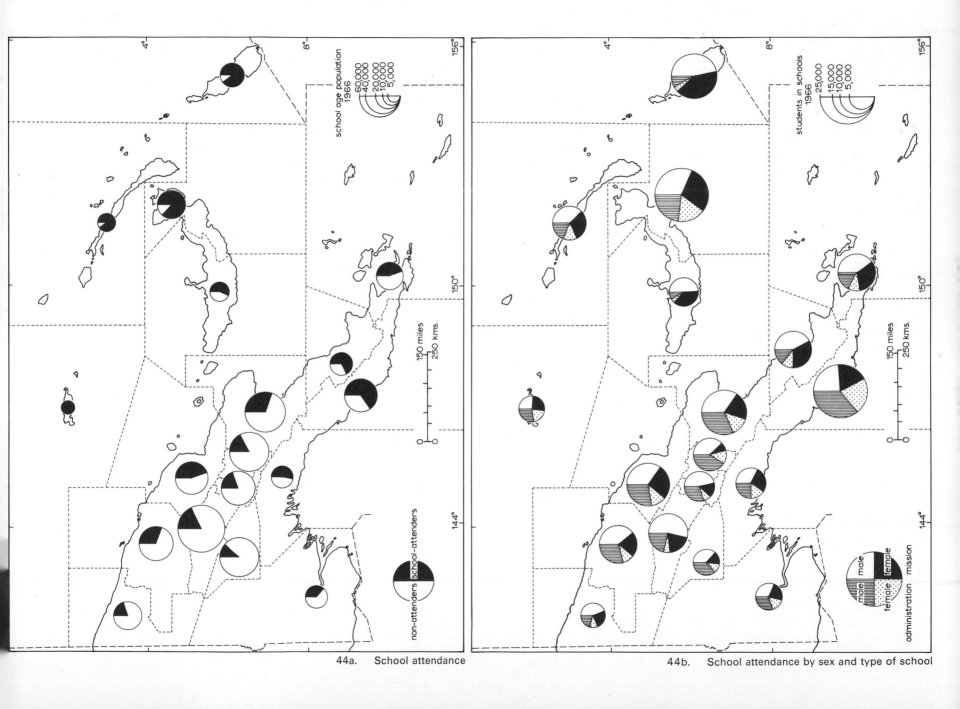

44a.   School attendance

44b.   School attendance by sex and type of school

ELECTORAL BOUNDARIES

The *Electoral Ordinance 1963–67* provides for a House of Assembly with most members elected by universal adult suffrage on a common roll. Voting by secret ballot is not compulsory and operates on a preferential system where the vote is valid even if only part of the voter's preference is shown. The first election was in 1964 and 10 members were elected from 'special' electorates, in which indigenes and expatriates could be enrolled but in which only expatriates could stand for election, and 44 members (of whom 38 were indigenes) were elected from 'open' electorates in which any resident could stand. In addition 10 members were chosen by the Administration.

Prior to the second elections in 1968, the composition of the House of Assembly was changed. The number of electorates was increased so that the population of open electorates was reduced from 45,000 to about 30,000 and the qualifications for election to the special or regional electorates, as they are now known, became an educational one—the possession of at least the Territory Intermediate Certificate or its equivalent. At present the House of Assembly has 94 members 10 nominated by the Administration; 15 elected from regional electorates and 69 from open electorates.

OPEN ELECTORATES

1. Kerowagi	24. Wapei-Nuku	47. Sumkar
2. Chimbu	25. Dreikikir	48. Mabuso
3. Sinasina	26. Maprik	49. Rai Coast
4. Gumine	27. Ambunti-Yangoru	50. Markham
5. Chuave	28. Wewak	51. Munya
6. Daulo	29. Angoram	52. Kabwum
7. Goroka	30. Lagaip	53. Nawae
8. Lufa	31. Wabag	54. Finschhafen
9. Henganofi	32. Wapenamanda	55. Huon Gulf
10. Okapa	33. Kompiam-Baiyer	56. Kaindi
11. Kainantu	34. Mul-Dei	57. North Fly
12. Manus	35. Jimi	58. South Fly
13. Kavieng	36. Hagen	59. Kikori
14. Namatanai	37. Wahgi	60. Kerema
15. Bougainville North	38. Kandep-Tambul	61. Hiri
16. Bougainville South	39. Nipa	62. Goilala
17. Talasea	40. Mendi	63. Moresby
18. Kandrian-Pomio	41. Kagua	64. Rigo-Abau
19. Gazelle	42. Ialibu	65. Sohe
20. Kokopo	43. Tari	66. Ijibatari
21. Rabaul	44. Koroba	67. Alotau
22. West Sepik Coastal	45. Bogia	68. Esa'Ala
23. Upper Sepik	46. Middle Ramu	69. Kula

REGIONAL ELECTORATES

A. Manus and New Ireland
B. Bougainville
C. West Sepik
D. East Sepik
E. Madang
F. East and West New Britain
G. Western Highlands
H. Chimbu
I. Eastern Highlands
J. Morobe
K. Southern Highlands
L. Western and Gulf
.M. Central
N. Northern
O. Milne Bay

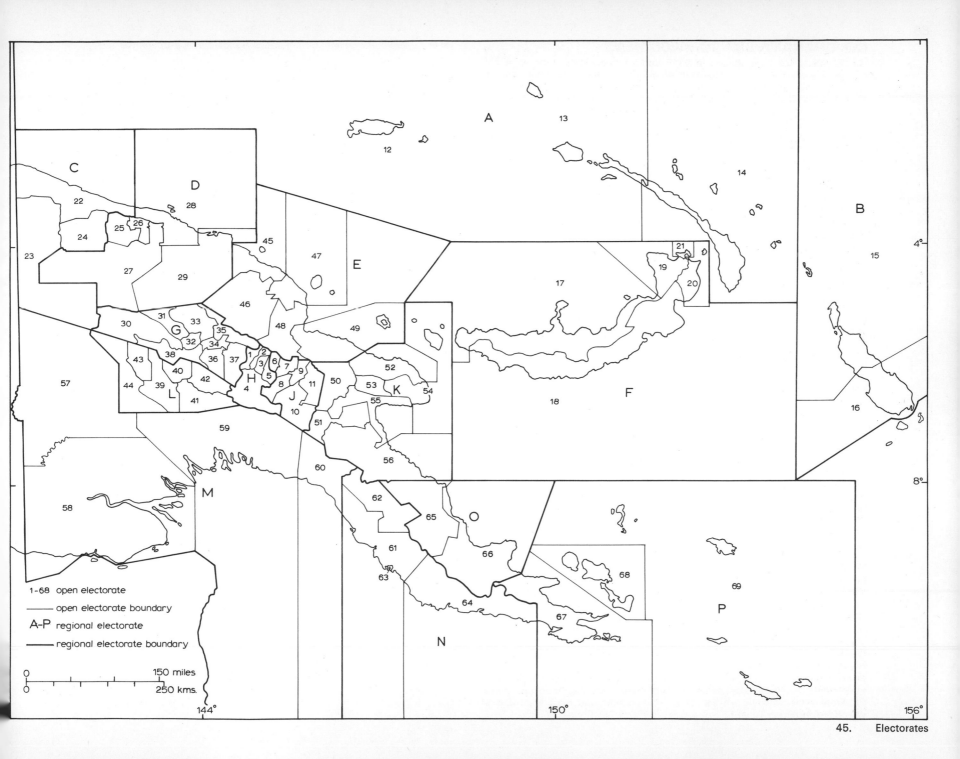

A
13
12
14
B
C
D
4°
22
28
26
45
25
47
24
23
27
29
E
19
21
20
15
46
48
17
F
31
33
35
G
32
34
49
30
1 2
38 36 37
3 6 7 9
43 40 H 5 8 11
44 39 42 4
L 41 10
57
52
50
53 K 54
55
18
16
51
8°
56
59
60
M
62
O
58
65
66
P
61
68
63
69
67 64
N
150 miles
250 kms.
144°
150°
156°

1-68 open electorate
—— open electorate boundary
A-P regional electorate
━━ regional electorate boundary

45.   Electorates

CO-OPERATIVES *JOHN RUMENS*

Co-operatives were introduced in 1948 and in January, 1969 there were 355 primary societies with a membership of about 110,000. The initial impetus resulted in a rapid growth of societies and membership up to 1954. Since then, there has been a relatively slow increase; shortage of adequate supervisory staff may have influenced policy, as the chief emphasis has been on consolidation.

Between 1958–59 and 1967–68 the number of co-operatives in the Papua region increased from 126 to 151 and membership from 21,000 to 26,500. However, total turnover rose from $807,000 to $1,464,000. Societies in the New Guinea Islands increased from 73 to 123 and although the rise in membership (25,000 to 30,000) was relatively small, turnover rose from $605,000 to $1,360,000. Co-operatives in the New Guinea Mainland region increased from 35 to 60 but membership rose from 27,000 to 53,000. Even more spectacular was the rise in turnover—from $223,000 to $2,599,000. This region has been the main growth area of the co-operative movement, which has provided the marketing facilities for the coffee grown by New Guineans. In the New Guinea Islands region, a substantial proportion of the increase in turnover has also resulted from the role of co-operatives in processing and marketing cocoa grown by members.

The Administration has made no financial contribution to the capital structure of the co-operative movement, but does provide registration and inspection services. These vital supervisory functions maintain the movement, despite apathy and lack of member loyalty in many areas.

The primary societies and their associations, which had been establishing themselves since 1948, formed regional unions in November, 1968. A month later, these regional unions created a national federation which then set up a wholesale society. Prior to the formation of the Papua and New Guinea Federation, Security, Finance and Shipping Societies, were developed as service societies for the Papuan Associations. At present they are *composite societies* jointly owned by the Federation, Unions and Associations. A possible development is for the Security Society and the Finance Society to be absorbed by the Papua and New Guinea Federation and be controlled in the same way as the Wholesale Society. In the case of the Shipping Society this appears unlikely.

The total turnover of primary societies in the year ending 31st March, 1968 was $5,400,000, of which $3,200,000 was generated by the processing and marketing of members' produce and the remaining 41 per cent by retailing operations. The New Guinea Mainland region accounted for $2,600,000 or 48 per cent of the total. Clearly this results from the presence in the region of the Chimbu Coffee Co-operative Limited which, with its turnover of $1,400,000 dominates the co-operative movement. In Papua, retailing operations account for approximately 66 per cent of total turnover whereas in the New Guinea Mainland region, producer servicing accounts for approximately 80 per cent of turnover. In the New Guinea Islands region, retailing and producer servicing functions are approximately equal in value.

Differences in the scale of operations in the three regions are reflected in the average size of membership of societies. In the New Guinea Mainland region, with the exception of the Madang District, the average membership exceeds 500—rising to 11,465 in the Chimbu Coffee Society. On the other hand, it is only in the Western District of the Papua region and the East New Britain District of the New Guinea Islands region that the average membership reaches or exceeds 500.

In order to provide facilities, such as cocoa fermentaries, Africultural Officers often start Rural Progress Societies, which are later registered as co-operatives. Producer societies handle a variety of commodities, the most important of which are shown in Table 1.

Table 1 *Value of Principal Commodities Handled by Co-operatives*

Commodity	Value Year Ended 31st March, 1968	Most Important Districts
Coffee	$1,612,400	Chimbu $1,125,000; Morobe $225,000; Sepik $147,500.
Copra	725,800	New Ireland $146,000; Milne Bay $126,000; Bougainville $110,000; Gulf $97,000.
Cacao	364,000	Bougainville $231,000; West New Britain $58,000; Northern $23,000; New Ireland $22,000; Madang $20,000.
Rice	130,000	Sepik $123,000; Madang $6,000.
Peanuts	106,000	Morobe $103,000; Eastern Highlands $3,000.
Crocodile skins	77,000	Western $63,000; Sepik $8,000; Gulf $6,000.
Timber	72,000	Gulf $69,000; Bougainville $3,000.
Fish	48,000	Central $46,000; Milne Bay $2,000.
Basketware	25,000	Bougainville $25,000.

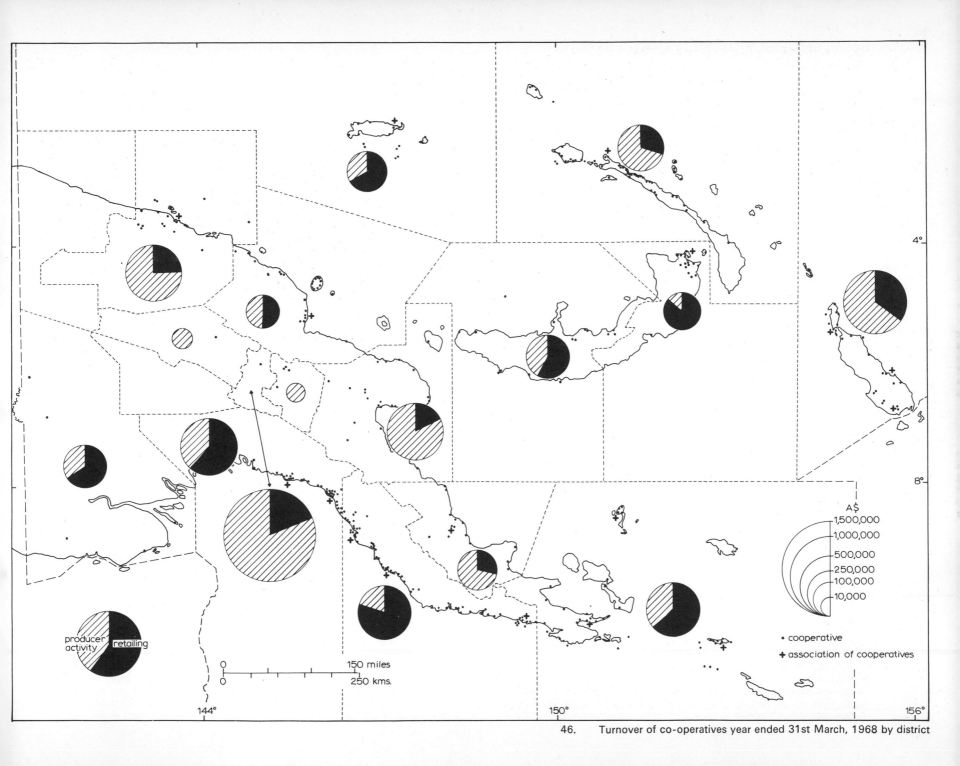

producer activity | retailing

A$
1,500,000
1,000,000
500,000
250,000
100,000
10,000

• cooperative
+ association of cooperatives

150 miles
250 kms.

144°   150°   156°
4°   8°

46.   Turnover of co-operatives year ended 31st March, 1968 by district

INDIGENOUSLY OWNED TRADE STORES
JOHN RUMENS

As the material used to compile this map represents the first attempt to gain an overall view of the number of indigenous trade store owners and the volume of business they transact, several caveats should be entered concerning the data. Firstly Administration field staff were requested to undertake the survey as an "extra", and, as records do not exist in the majority of stores, annua sales had to be estimated on the basis of stock on hand and cash takings for several days by people who, in many cases were not skilled in making such estimates. Subsequently Business Advisory Officers in the Rabaul and Port Moresby areas, who have been helping keep records for some trade store owners, have discovered significantly larger sales for certain stores in these areas. Although it is known that there has been a very rapid rise (up to 100 per cent) in sales in some non-indigenous stores in the same areas in the intervening time, it is likely that some underestimating did occur. Also this is not the full measure of retailing undertaken by indigenously owned businesses as co-operatives and corporate organizations, such as Namasu and Waso, are significant. Additionally it should be borne in mind that sales in the markets found in all urban centres, together with sales direct to householders, government institutions and plantations of foodstuffs, firewood, artefacts, etc., are not included. Most of these sales by indigenous entrepreneurs would, if handled by non-indigenous businessmen, take place in a more "formal" store situation. Therefore the trade store survey cannot be directly compared with surveys of non-indigenous retailing activities.

The character of the stores varies greatly—from a walled-off portion of the house, often seen in Hanuabada, through tiny roadside structures which are a feature along parts of the Highland Highway, to quite impressive buildings such as the one recently financed by the Development Bank in Tupusereia. The range in size of annual turnover of trade stores is remarkable—from $48,000 recorded for a store in Telefomin down to $5·00 for a store in the Abau sub-district. The Telefomin store, located in one of the least developed areas of the Territory, is registered in the name of an indigenous proprietor—however it receives a considerable amount of guidance, and business, from the local mission. To the proprietors of many of the smaller stores their operation is more of a status symbol than a profit-seeking venture. Consequently large numbers of them fail.

The survey required an estimate of the degree of dependence on the earnings of the trade store: thus it was necessary to enquire into the other activities of the owners. The findings showed that many trade store owners engaged in other activities and have experience of working outside the village milieu in the modern economy. For example many successful trade store proprietors have a trucking operation, or substantial plantings of cash crops, or are involved in a cattle project whilst many public servants have trade stores registered in the name of a member of their family.

The expected pattern of store activity would be a high volume of business in the urban and peri-urban areas and those rural areas where transport networks and cash cropping are well developed, with a decline in volume occurring as accessibility becomes more difficult and the level of participation in the cash economy decreases. In general this is the case as the twelve sub-districts with the highest annual turnover, in descending order, are Port Moresby, Rabaul, Kukipi, Madang, Mt. Hagen, Goroka, Lae, Kerema, Kokopo, Gumine, Minj and Popondetta. Kukipi and Kerema are the only two sub-districts that appear anomalous. Although there is relatively little primary production in these sub-districts both have ready access to Port Moresby, and remittances from the large number of workers who have migrated to the urban centres could help sustain this high level of turnover.

At the other end of the scale, no indigenously owned trade stores were reported in the Morehead, Nomad, Wonenara and Losuia sub-districts and the eight sub-districts with the lowest annual turnover, in ascending order, were Kiunga, Lake Kopiago, Mendi, Nipa, Pomio, Menyamya, Koroba and Kandrian. The absence of privately owned trade stores in Losuia seems strange when the level of co-operative activity is noted. Mendi's lower ranking than Nipa and Koroba sub-districts, for which there is no apparent explanation, upsets the "centre/periphery" pattern. The strong relationship between transport and economic activity is strikingly illustrated by the relatively high level of turnover in all sub-districts through which the Highlands Highway passes.

While in every sub-district per capita expenditure in indigenously owned stores is quite low, and the $3 million turnover of the 6,500 stores constitutes a small proportion of total retail activity, these enterprises do represent significant participation in the tertiary sector of the exchange economy by Papuans and New Guineans. A proposal, aimed at increasing the indigenous share of retailing activity, is that trade stores licences (among other things) should only be issued to Papuans and New Guineans. Adoption of such a proposal, which has many ramifications, would require significant changes in present policy as expressed in *"Programs and Policies"*—the economic development plan.

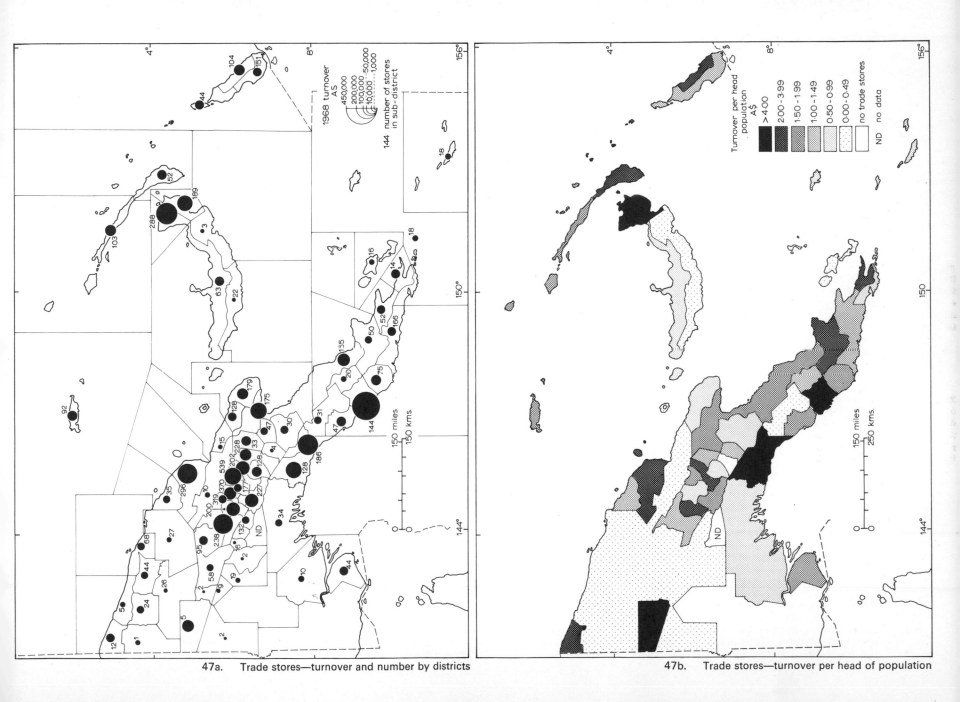

47a.   Trade stores—turnover and number by districts

47b.   Trade stores—turnover per head of population

ACCOMMODATION AND TOURISM
JANETTA SMITH *

During the last four years Papua and New Guinea has more than doubled its tourist intake from 10,444 in 1965 to over 23,500 for the year ending June 30, 1969. To keep pace with this increase of over 20 per cent per annum, accommodation in all towns in the Territory has been expanded and improved. Hotels in the major towns of Port Moresby, Lae, Madang, Wewak, Mt. Hagen, Goroka and Rabaul are small but modern, offering private facilities in most bedrooms and air-conditioning in coastal areas. Guest-houses are generally unlicensed premises offering cheaper accommodation and meals. Smaller hotels and guest-homes offering fewer facilities are located in more isolated areas.

It is projected that by late 1971 over 700 hotel rooms will be added to the existing 1,270 rooms in Papua and New Guinea. Probably the most interesting development will be the building of international resort hotels incorporating native building materials in their construction. Such resort hotels are planned for the Bougainville, Sepik and Highlands areas.

Thousands of tourists come each year to witness the Highlands Shows in Mt. Hagen and Goroka. The Sepik River area is emerging as a major tourist destination with tours on house-boats along the river, visiting villages and "Haus Tambarans" or Cult Houses. The Trobriand Islands to the east of Papua, famous for its yam festival, intricate carvings and the mini grass skirts worn by the Trobriand women, are of considerable interest to the visitor.

Papua and New Guinea offers the visitor a wide range of interests, from the orchids and animals to the ancient crafts of the people. Active volcanoes, particularly near Rabaul, and the famous Birds of Paradise, a collection of which are in the Baiyer River Sanctuary near Mt. Hagen, are other major attractions. In addition, increasing numbers of veterans from World War II are returning to their battlefields with wives and children to discover the many changes which have occurred since 1945.

Papua and New Guinea is one of the last countries in the Pacific to recognize its tourist potential and will need much more investment in accommodation and services if tourism is to increase at the rate equivalent to that experienced by other Pacific island territories.

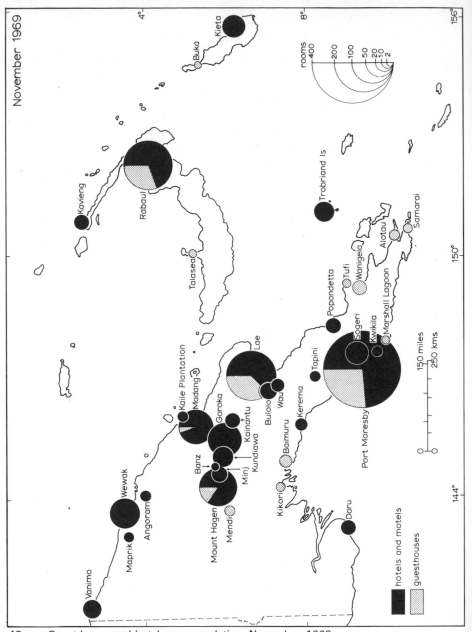

November 1969

48. Guest house and hotel accommodation, November, 1969

* Projects Officer, Department of Trade and Industry, Port Moresby.

INTENSIVE ETHNOGRAPHIC STUDIES
RALPH BULMER *

This map locates traditional societies which have been the subject of intensive ethnographic enquiries, in the main by professional anthropologists. Sociological research concentrating on non-traditional institutions or forms of grouping has not been included, as also ethnographic survey work, whether by brief visits to individual communities or by relatively systematic coverage of large areas (e.g. Seligmann's classic survey of the coastal and highland peoples of S.E. Papua in 1904, or C. A. Schmitz's survey of the Huon Peninsula in 1955/6). A great deal of ethnography, some of it of high quality, undertaken by missionaries, administration officials and other non-professional research workers, has also been omitted, though studies in this category which have resulted in academic monographs or substantial publication in learned journals have in general been included. With the above limitations, nearly all studies commenced up to 1968 have been included. Of studies commenced in 1969 only those that had been completed or had continued for a minimum period of six months by November, 1969 are included.

Sources which may be consulted for details of individual projects and resulting publications include: Elkin, A. P., 1953, *Social Anthropology in Melanesia*, Melbourne; Dept. of Anthropology and Sociology, Australian National University, 1968, *Ethnographic Bibliography of New Guinea*, Canberra Reeves, S. & Dudley, M., 1969, *Research and Publications, Papua–New Guinea, 1962–67*, New Guinea Research Bulletin, No. 32, Canberra; Dept. of Anthropology and Sociology, University of Papua and New Guinea, 1968–69, *Man in New Guinea*, Vol. 1, Nos. 1–4.

KEY TO RESEARCH WORKERS

1. Armstrong, W. E. — Rossel Island, Milne Bay D., 1921.
2. Aufenanger, H. — Gende of Bundi, Madang D., 1934–38.
3. Barth, F. — Baktamin (Faiwol speakers), nr. Oslobip, Western D., 1968.
4. Bateson, G. — Istmul, E. Sepik D., 1929, 1930, 1932–33, 1938.
5. Bell, F. L. S. — Boieng, Tanga, New Ireland D., 1933.
6. Belshaw, C. S. — Motu of Hanuabada, Central D., 1950–51.
7. Berndt, R. M., & C. H. — Usarufa, Kamano, Jate and North Fore, E. Highlands D., 1951–52, 1952–53, 1964.
8. Billings, D. — Mangai, New Ireland D., 1966–67.
9. Blackwood, B. M. — Petats of Buka and Kurtachi of N. Bougainville, Bougainville D., 1929–30.
10. Blackwood, B. M. — Nauti and Ekuti (Anga or "Kukukuku") of Upper Watut, Morobe D., 1936–37.
11. Bowers, N. — Kakoli of Upper Kaugel Valley, W. Highlands D., 1962–63, 1968–69.
12. Braggington, J. — Bena, N. of Mt. Lufa, E. Highlands D., 1968–69.
13. Brandewie, E. — Kumai-Enganoi (Melpa or Mbowamb), W. Highlands D., 1963–65.

— Brookfield, H. C. — See 14.
14. Brown, P. (P. Brown Glick), & Brookfield, H. C. — Naregu tribe, Chimbu, Chimbu D., 1958–60 and subs.
15. Bulmer, R. N. H. — Kyaka Enga of Baiyer Valley, W. Highlands D., 1955–56, 1959.
16. Bulmer, R. N. H. — Karam of Upper Kaironk Valley, Madang D., 1960, 1963–64 and subs.
17. Burridge, K. O. L. — Tangu, Madang D., 1952.
— Chowning, A. — Lakalai. See 43.
18. Chowning, A. — Molima, Fergusson Is., Milne Bay D., 1957–58.
19. Chowning, A. — Kombe (Kove), Talasea, W. New Britain D., 1966, 1968, 1969.
— Chowning, A. — Sengseng. See 42.
20. Clarke, W. C., & Street, J. — Maring, esp. Bomagai-Angoiang of Sipopi, W. Highlands and Madang D., 1964–65.
21. Cook, E. A. — Narak, Jimi Valley, W. Highlands D., 1961–63.
22. Craig, R., & B. — Telefomin, W. Sepik D., 1962–65 and subs.
23. Criper, C. — Upper Chimbu, Chimbu D., 1962–64.
24. Crocombe, R. G., Hogbin, G. R., Rimoldi, M., & others — Orokaiva, Northern D., 1962–66.
25. Dark, P. J. C., & Gerbrands, A. A. — Kilenge, Cape Gloucester, W. New Britain D., 1964, 1966–67.
26. Dornstreich, M. — Gadio Enga, E. Sepik D., 1967–68.
27. Du Toit, B. M. — Gadsup of Akuna Village, E. Highlands D., 1961–62.
28. Epstein, A. L., & T. S. — Tolai of Matupit, E. New Britain D., 1960–61, 1967–68.
29. Errington, F., & S. — Duke of York Is., E. New Britain D., 1968.
30. Fischer, H. — Lower Watut (Bentseng Village), Morobe D., 1958, 1959.
31. Fischer, H. — Yeghuje Anga ("Kukukuku"), Upper Tauri River, Gulf D., 1958–59, 1965.
32. Forge, J. A. W. — Abelam, E. Sepik D., 1958–59, 1962–63.
33. Fortune, R. F. — Dobu of Tewara and Dobu Is., Milne Bay D., 1927–28.
— Fortune, R. F. — Manus. See 75.
— Fortune, R. F. — Arapesh. See 76.
— Fortune, R. F. — Mundugumor. See 77.
— Fortune, R. F. — Tchambuli. See 78.
34. Fortune, R. F. — Kamano of E. Highlands D., 1935 and subs.
35. Freedman, M. — Mandok, Siassi Is., Morobe D., 1965–66.
36. Gell, A. — Waina-Sowanda, nr. Imonda, W. Sepik D., 1969–.
— Gerbrands, A. A. — Kilenge. See 25.
37. Girard, F. — Buang of Snake River, Morobe D., 1954–55.
38. Glasse, R. M. — Huli of Tari, S. Highlands D., 1955–56, 1959.
39. Glasse, R. M., & Glasse, S. (S. Lindenbaum) — Southern Fore, E. Highlands D., 1961–63.
40. Glick, L. B. — Gimi of Hegetura, E. Highlands D., 1960–62.
— Glick, P. Brown — Chimbu. See 14.
41. Godelier, M. — Baruya Anga ("Kukukuku") nr. Wonenara, E. Highlands D., 1967–69.

* Professor of Anthropology and Sociology, University of Papua and New Guinea.

42. Goodale, J., & Chowning, A.   Kaulong and Sengseng, W. New Britain D., 1962, 1963–64 and subs.
43. Goodenough, W., Chowning, A., & Valentine, C. A.   Lakalai (West Nakanai), E. New Britain D., 1953–56 and subs.
44. Gorlin, P.   Abelam, E. Sepik D., 1969.
— Gostin, O.   See 100.
45. Groves, M. C.   Motu, esp. of Manumanu Village, Central D., 1953–54 and subs.
46. Groves, W. C.   Tatau Village, Tabar Is., New Ireland D., 1933.
47. Harding, T. G.   Sio and Siassi, Morobe D., 1963–64.
48. Hatanaka, S.   Sismin (Saiyolof Hewa), nr. Oksapmin, W. Sepik D., 1967–68.
49. Heintze, D.   Fisoa, New Ireland D., 1967–68.
— Hogbin, G. R.   Orokaiva. See 24.
50. Hogbin, H. I.   Wogeo Is., E. Sepik D., 1934.
51. Hogbin, H. I.   Busama, Morobe D., 1944–50.
52. Hogg, L.   Amenob L.G.C. area, Madang D., 1968–69.
— Jablonko, A., & M.   Maring. See 123.
53. Jackson, G. G.   Kobon of Yhar, Lower Kaironk Valley, Madang D., 1966–68 and subs.
54. Jenness, D.   Bwaidogu, Milne Bay D., 1911–12.
55. Kaberry, P.   Abelam, E. Sepik D., 1939–40.
56. Kelly, R.   Etoro, nr. Komo, Western D., 1968–69.
57. Keysser, C.   Kai, Morobe D., 1899–1910.
58. Landtman, G.   Kiwai, Western D., 1910–12.
59. Langlas, C.   Foe, Lake Kutubu, S. Highlands D., 1965–66, 1968.
60. Langness, L. L.   Bena, E. Highlands D., 1961–62.
61. Lawrence, P.   Garia, Madang D., 1949–50, 1953 and subs.
62. Lawrence, P.   Ngaiang, Madang D., 1953, 1956.
63. Lea, D. A. M.   Abelam, E. Sepik D., 1961 and subs.
64. Lehner, S.   Bukaua, Morobe D., 1906–10 and subs.
65. Leininger, M.   Gadsup, E. Highlands D., 1963–64.
66. Lewis, G.   Gnau of Rauit, W. Sepik D., 1968–69.
67. Lewis, P. H.   Lesu and Libba, New Ireland D., 1953–54.
— Lindenbaum, S.   S. Fore. See 39.
68. Luzbetak, L.   Banz, Middle Wahgi, W. Highlands D., 1950s.
69. McArthur, M.   Kunimaipa, Central D., 1953–57, 1968.
70. McLaren, P. L., & G. J.   Bongu-Rereu, Rai Coast, Madang D., 1968–69 and cont.
71. McSwain, R.   Karkar Is., Madang D., 1966–67, 1968–69.
72. Maher, R. F.   Purari Delta, Gulf D., 1955.
73. Malinowski, B. M.   Mailu, Central D., 1915.
74. Malinowski, B. M.   Kiriwina, Trobriand Is., Milne Bay D., 1915–18.
75. Mead, M., & Fortune, R. F.   Manus of Peri Village, Manus D., 1928–29, 1953 and subs.
76. Mead, M., & Fortune, R. F.   Arapesh, esp. of Alitoa Village, E. Sepik D., 1931, 1936.
77. Mead, M., & Fortune, R. F.   Mundugumor, of Yuat R., E. Sepik D., 1932.
78. Mead, M., & Fortune, R. F.   Tchambuli (Chambri), E. Sepik D., 1933.

79. Meggitt, M. J.   Mae Enga, W. Highlands D., 1955–57.
80. Miclouho-Maclay, N. N.   Bongu, Rai Coast, Madang D., 1871–72, 1876–77.
81. Morren, G.   Miyanmin, W. Sepik D., 1967–69.
82. Nelson, H.   Kaimbi, Nebilyer Valley, W. Highlands D., 1967–69.
83. Neuhaus, K.   Pala (Namatanai), New Ireland D., 1910–19 and subs. to 1942.
84. Newman, P. L.   Gururumba of Miruma, E. Highlands D., 1959–60.
85. Newman, P. L.   Awa, E. Highlands D., 1964–65.
86. Nieuwenhuijsen, J. Van   Suki, Western D., 1963–65.
87. Nilles, J.   Chimbu (Kuman), Chimbu D., 1937–42 and subs.
88. Ogan, E.   Nasioi of Aropa Valley, Bougainville D., 1966–67.
89. Oliver, D. L.   Siuai, Bougainville D., 1938–39.
90. Oram, N.   Vulaa (Hula), Central D., 1964–65.
91. Panoff, M., & F.   Maenge, E. New Britain D., 1966–68 and subs.
92. Perry, A.   Oksapmin, W. Sepik D., 1967–68.
93. Powdermaker, H.   Lesu, New Ireland D., 1929–30.
94. Powell, H. A.   Kiriwina, Trobriand Is., Milne Bay D., 1950–51.
95. Ramstad, Y.   Lihir, New Ireland D., 1968–69.
96. Rappaport, R. A.   Maring of Tsembaga, Simbai Valley, Madang D., 1962–63.
97. Read, K. E.   Ngarawapum (Atzera-speakers), Morobe D., 1944.
98. Read, K. E.   Gahuku-Gama, E. Highlands D., 1950–52.
99. Reay, M.   Kuma of Minj, Wahgi Valley, W. Highlands D., 1953–55, 1963 and subs.
— Reed, S. W.   Kwoma. See 131.
100. Rijswijck, O. (Gostin, O.)   Kuni of Bakioudu, Central D., 1963–65.
— Rimoldi, M.   Orokaiva. See 24.
101. Rimoldi, M.   Buka, Bougainville D., 1965–66 and subs.
102. Robbins, S.   Auyana, E. Highlands D., 1962–63.
103. Roheim, D.   Duau (Dobu), Normanby Is., Milne Bay D., 1930.
104. Rowe, W.   Mbowamb (Melpa), W. Highlands D., 1966–67, 1968.
105. Ryan, D'A. J.   Mendi, S. Highlands D., 1954, 1955–56.
106. Ryan, D.   Elema (Toaripi) of Kukipi, Gulf D., 1961–62 and subs.
107. Salisbury, R. F.   Siane, E. Highlands D., 1952–53, 1967.
108. Salisbury, R. F.   Tolai, E. New Britain D., 1957, 1962 and subs.
109. Sankoff, G.   Buang of Mumeng, Morobe D., 1966–67, 1968.
110. Schieffelin, E. L.   Kaluli, Mt. Bosavi, Western D., 1966–68.
111. Schlesier, E.   Me'udana, Normanby Is., Milne Bay D., 1961–62.
112. Schmitz, C.   Wantoat, Morobe D., 1955–56.
113. Schwartz, T., & L.   Manus Is., Manus D., 1953–54 and subs.
114. Schwimmer, E. G.   Orokaiva, Northern D., 1966–67.

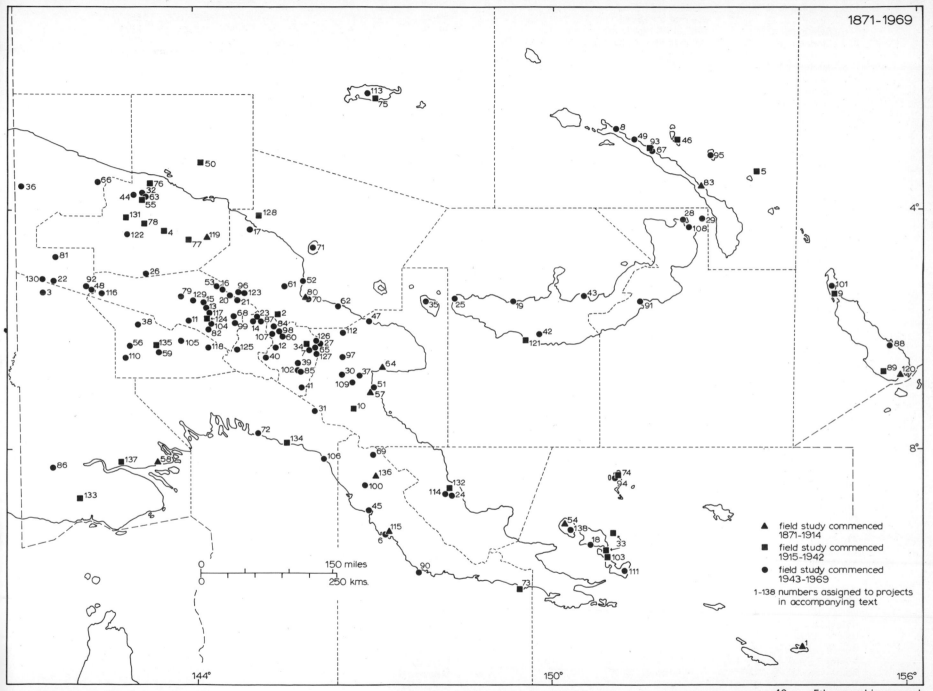

field study commenced
1871-1914

field study commenced
1915-1942

field study commenced
1943-1969

1-138 numbers assigned to projects
in accompanying text

150 miles

250 kms.

49.　　Ethnographic research

115. Seligmann, C. G.   Koita and Motu of Port Moresby region, Central D., 1904.
116. Steadman, L. B.   Hewa, W. Highlands D., 1967–69.
117. Strathern, A. J., & A. M. Mbowamb (Melpa), W. Highlands D., 1964–65, 1967–68 and subs.
118. Strathern, A. J.   Wiru, Pangia, S. Highlands D., 1967–68 and cont.
—   Strauss, H.   Mbowamb. See 124.
—   Street, J.   Maring. See 20.

119. Thurnwald, R.   Banaro, Keram R., E. Sepik D., 1912–15.
120. Thurnwald, R., & H.   Buin, Bougainville D., 1908, 1933–34.
121. Todd, J. A.   Moewehafen, W. New Britain D., 1933, 1935.
122. Townsend, P. K., & W.   Saino, Wogamush R., W. Sepik D., 1966–67.
—   Valentine, C. A.   Lakalai. See 43.
123. Vayda, A. P., & C., &   Maring of Gunts, Lower Simbai Valley, Jablonko, A., & M.   Madang D., 1962–63, 1966 and subs.
124. Vicedom, G. F., &   Mbowamb (Melpa), W. Highlands D., Strauss, H.   1934–67.
125. Wagner, R.   Daribi, Karimui, Chimbu D., 1963–65, 1968–69.
126. Watson, J. B., & V.   Agarabi, E. Highlands D., 1953–54.
127. Watson, J. B., & V.   Tairora, E. Highlands D., 1953–54, 1959, 1963–64.
128. Wedgwood, C. H.   Manam Is., Madang D., 1933.
129. Westermann, T.   Laiapu (Raiapu) Enga, W. Highlands D., 1965–68.
130. Wheatcroft, W.   Tifalmin, W. Sepik D., 1969 and cont.
131. Whiting, J. W. M., &   Kwoma, E. Sepik D., 1936–37. Reed, S. W.
132. Williams, F. E.   Orokaiva, Northern D., 1923–25.
133. Williams, F. E.   Keraki of Trans-Fly, Western D., 1926–32.
134. Williams, F. E.   Elema of Orokolo, Gulf D., 1923–37.
135. Williams, F. E.   Foe of Lake Kutubu, S. Highlands D., 1938–39.
136. Williamson, R. W.   Mafulu, Central D., 1910.
137. Wirz, P.   Gogodara (Gogodala), Western D., 1930.
138. Young, M.   Kaluana and Bwaidogu of Goodenough Is., Milne Bay D., 1966–67, 1968.

INDEX OF SOCIETIES

EXCAVATIONS OF PREHISTORIC SITES
JIM ALLEN *

Before 1959 the only significant contribution made by archaeology to the history of Papua and New Guinea was the recovery of a human skull from river gravels near Aitape in 1929. Although thought then to be of Pleistocene age, recent research has indicated that it is only 4,000–5,000 years old. The period of man's first entry is not yet known. However, on Southeast Asian and Australian evidence an antiquity of perhaps 50,000 years has been suggested. The earliest C14 date so far is from Kosipe, an open site in the Papuan highlands which man may have first visited c. 26,000 years ago, although the date still requires some verification.

The most concerted research has been in the Highlands, where the earliest dates associated with man come from Kiowa (10,350±140 B.P.) and Kafiavana (10,730±370 B.P.). Warmer conditions towards the end of the Pleistocene may have enabled hunter/gatherer groups to move into the area. They occupied caves and rockshelters, manufactured stone and presumably wooden tools and weapons, and exploited natural food sources. There is evidence of some local differentiation between eastern and western groups. Marine shell in some sites 9,000 years ago indicates that trading systems were developed early in Highlands history.

Beginning about 6,000 years ago some cultural changes have been documented, particularly the presence of pigs, which may indicate the presence of rudimentary root-crop horticulture, even allowing that hunting and gathering remained the economic base. Such horticulture would exclude the present staple, sweet potato, which appears to have an antiquity in New Guinea of only 300 to 400 years. The earliest positive evidence for horticulture comes from the Manton site where, at least 2,500 years ago complex water-channels were dug, presumably for drainage. Excavations recovered wooden digging sticks, a paddle-shaped spade and polished stone axe-adzes very similar to those in use in the area this century.

Most lowland sites listed are still being investigated. However, Watom Island has produced a date of c. 2,500 years ago for the presence of a distinctively decorated pottery called Lapita. Found at a number of sites between New Guinea and Tonga, it may be associated with man's first entry into Polynesia. Trial excavations at Ou-Ou Creek have revealed a sealed pre-ceramic layer below pottery deposits. It is hoped that this site will yield an early date for lowland occupation. Prehistoric coastal population may well prove to have been quite dense; in the immediate surrounds of Port Moresby alone, surveys have so far located some 70 sites.

Bibliography:
Bulmer, S., 1966. *The Prehistory of the New Guinea Highlands,* unpubl., M.A. Thesis, University of Auckland.
White, J. P., 1967. *Taim Bilong Bipo: Investigations Towards a Prehistory of the Papua–New Guinea Highlands,* unpubl., Ph.D. Thesis, Australian National University.

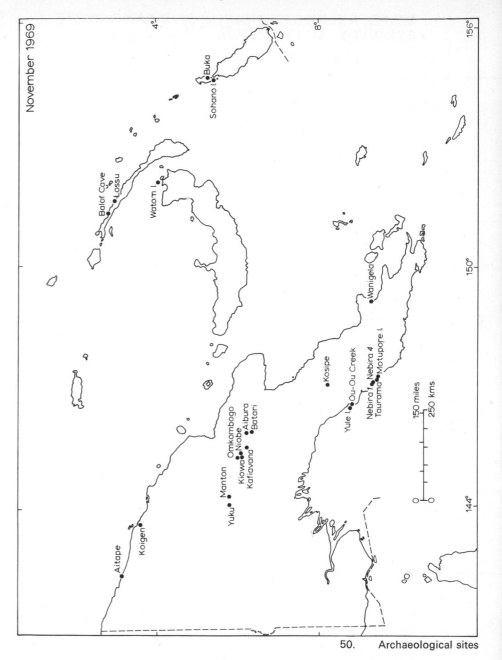

November 1969

50.　　Archaeological sites

* Lecturer in Anthropology and Sociology, University of Papua and New Guinea.

MAPS, AIR PHOTOGRAPHS AND LAND SYSTEM REPORTS *M. J. F. BROWN*

Many topographic maps of Papua and New Guinea are of a very poor quality. Most are at small scales, are generally inaccurate and must be used with a great deal of caution.

The most complete coverage of the Territory is by maps at a scale of 1 :1,000,000. The Australian Geographical Series (A.G.S.) and the World Aeronautical Chart (W.A.C.) contain the same basic information, the latter having superimposed aeronautical data. At the same scale are maps of the U.S.A.F. Operational Navigation Chart (O.N.C.) series which give a coverage of the whole Territory and of Irian Barat. Although compiled from the same basic information as the A.G.S. series these are visually superior maps. Relief is indicated by hill shading and contours, and information presented with great clarity. As in the A.G.S. series no contours are shown for parts of the Highlands. A more specialized series is that of the Road System of Papua and New Guinea which distinguishes the various classes of roads and portrays only a limited amount of topographic information.

The 1 :250,000 maps give the widest coverage at the largest scale but are often inaccurate. They are based on a variety of sources some dating to pre-War times. Many carry a red overprint showing road, track and village information revised in or after 1966. There is a complete coverage of the mainland, except for the Port Moresby sheet, but New Ireland and Manus are the only off-shore islands covered.

Reconnaissance maps of the western border area at 1 :100,000 are available in the Border (Special) series (2nd Ed., 1963). These show drainage, villages and tracks, while relief is depicted by hill-shading. No heights are given. Military Survey maps at a scale of 1 :63,360 were published during the war and cover most coastal areas of mainland New Guinea, eastern Papua, and the whole of New Britain. These maps are not generally available for purchase.

Accurate topographic·maps at a scale of 1 :50,000 are available for a limited area adjacent to Port Moresby, and less reliable coverage at the same scale is available for New Ireland and Bougainville. Preliminary Detail Plots 1 :50,000 have been published for parts of the Western Highlands and the Port Moresby region. These are uncontrolled, uncontoured, and show no heights but depict relief by hill-shading. Drainage, villages and tracks are shown. Maps published by the U.S. Army give full coverage of Manus at 1 :25,000.

Aerial Photography. Owing to the general inadequacy of topographic maps in the Territory great reliance must often be placed on aerial photographs. Photomaps, at approximately 1 :63,360, are available for most of eastern Papua and mainland New Guinea. Western Papua is not well covered and none are available for the island areas.

These are essentially an assemblage of air photographs and provide a key for the CAJ series photography taken for the Division of National Mapping. Coverage of aerial photographs in the CAJ series outside the areas for which photomaps are available is shown in Map 51a. Various other agencies, notably QASCO, have carried out aerial photography for specialized purposes in many areas and there is also aerial photography taken during World War II. Copies of most air photographs of Papua and New Guinea are held in the Department of Forests, Port Moresby and may be readily inspected.

The Land Research Division, C.S.I.R.O., have carried out land system surveys of much of Papua and New Guinea. Published reports exist for much of the coastal area of eastern Papua, the Wewak-Lower Sepik area, the Wabag-Tari area and for Bougainville. Reports that are in press or mimeographed cover the Mount Hagen-Goroka, Ramu valley and Madang areas and the Fly river area adjacent to the western border. Further reports are in preparation for the remainder of the Sepik coastal area and for eastern Papua.

Availability

The following maps may be obtained from the Division of National Mapping, Canberra: 1 :1,000,000 A.G.S. and W.A.C. series; 1 :250,000; 1 :50,000, Preliminary Detail Plots and the 1 :100,000 Border series. The U.S.A.F. (O.N.C.) 1 :1,000,000 series is obtainable from the Aeronautical Chart and Information Center, U.S.A.F., St. Louis, Mo.63118. Most maps may also be obtained through Plan Drawing Service, Box 593, Port Moresby. The Photomaps and aerial photographs of the CAJ series are obtainable from the Division of National Mapping. Photographs by QASCO may be obtained from QASCO Air Surveys, Box 1395, Boroko. C.S.I.R.O. reports may be obtained from the Division of Land Research, Canberra.

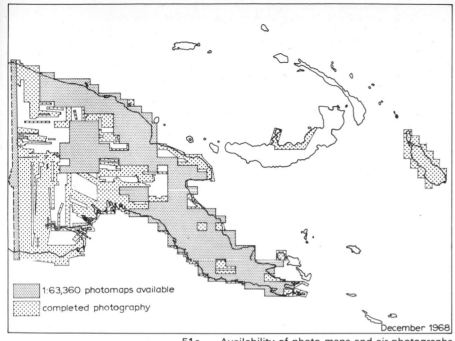

1:63,360 photomaps available

completed photography

December 1968

51a.　Availability of photo maps and air photographs

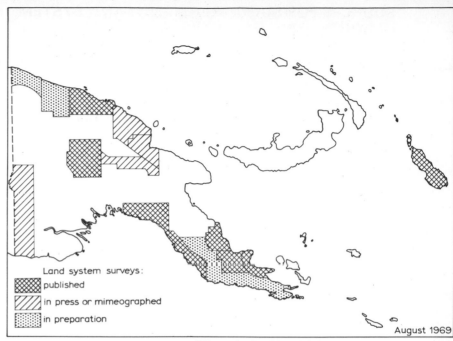

Land system surveys:

published

in press or mimeographed

in preparation

August 1969

51b.　Availability of C.S.I.R.O. land system reports

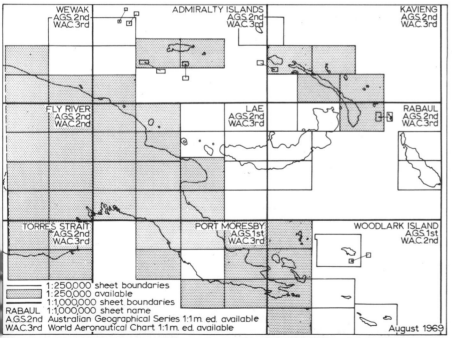

WEWAK
A.G.S.2nd
W.A.C.3rd

ADMIRALTY ISLANDS
A.G.S.2nd
W.A.C.3rd

KAVIENG
A.G.S.2nd
W.A.C.3rd

FLY RIVER
A.G.S.2nd
W.A.C.2nd

LAE
A.G.S.2nd
W.A.C.3rd

RABAUL
A.G.S.2nd
W.A.C.3rd

TORRES STRAIT
A.G.S.2nd
W.A.C.3rd

PORT MORESBY
A.G.S.1st
W.A.C.3rd

WOODLARK ISLAND
A.G.S.1st
W.A.C.2nd

1:250,000 sheet boundaries
1:250,000 available
1:1,000,000 sheet boundaries
RABAUL　1:1,000,000 sheet name
A.G.S.2nd　Australian Geographical Series 1:1m. ed. available
W.A.C.3rd　World Aeronautical Chart 1:1m. ed. available

August 1969

51c.　Availability of 1 : 250.000 and 1 : 1,000.000 maps

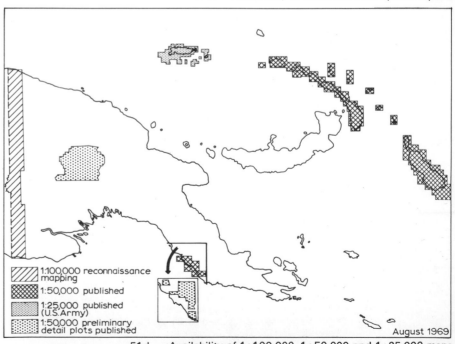

1:100,000 reconnaissance mapping

1:50,000 published

1:25,000 published (U.S.Army)

1:50,000 preliminary detail plots published

August 1969

51d.　Availability of 1 : 100.000, 1 : 50.000 and 1 : 25.000 maps

SOURCES FOR MAPS